HOW TO MAKE IT BIG
AS A CONSULTANT

Other Books by William A. Cohen

Principles of Technical Management
(AMACOM, 1980)

How to Sell to the Government (John Wiley &
Sons, Inc., 1981)

Successful Marketing for Small Business (with
Marshall Reddick, AMACOM, 1981)

*The Entrepreneur and Small Business Problem-
Solver: An Encyclopedia Reference and Guide*
(John Wiley & Sons, Inc., 1983)

The Executive's Guide to Finding a Superior Job,
rev. ed. (AMACOM, 1983)

Direct Response Marketing (John Wiley & Sons,
Inc., 1984)

*Top Executive Performance: Eleven Keys to
Success and Power* (with Nurit Cohen, John
Wiley & Sons, Inc., 1984)

*Building a Mail Order Business: A Complete
Manual for Success*, 2nd ed. (John Wiley &
Sons, Inc., 1985)

William A. Cohen

HOW TO MAKE IT BIG
AS A CONSULTANT

AMERICAN MANAGEMENT ASSOCIATION

Library of Congress Cataloging in Publication Data

Cohen, William A., 1937–
    How to make it big as a consultant.

    Bibliography: p.
    Includes index.
    1. Business consultants.   I. Title.
HD69.C6C57   1985   658.4'6   85-47678
ISBN 0-8144-5821-1

Printing number

10 9 8 7 6 5 4 3 2 1

306304

This book is dedicated to the memory of my father
Sidney Oliver Cohen
who, even on his deathbed, never failed to give excellent
counseling and advice whenever it was requested.

PREFACE

I didn't start out in life to become a business consultant. I know that I am not alone in this, for I have talked to hundreds of other consultants, both full- and part-time, and very few started out with that intention. Most of them must have had an early experience like mine. Because my entrance into the consulting field was unplanned, the first time I performed consulting services I had no one to ask for advice.

Experience in other fields had taught me that whenever I lacked knowledge about something, my first step should be to find a book on the subject. So I went to do just that. I visited several bookstores; I checked with the libraries. But I found few books with the information I needed. How much should I charge? Was a contract absolutely necessary? Did I need a business license or some other kind of license? What could I do as a part-time consultant without running into a conflict of interest with my full-time employer? How much could I make if I decided to devote full time to consulting? Also, if I consulted full time, how much time would I need to spend marketing my services versus actual consulting, and how should I go about marketing my services, anyway? I was plagued by these and numerous other questions, but I had nowhere to turn for answers.

Eventually I learned, but mainly it was the hard way—through experience. I made numerous mistakes, which in some cases cost me money and in all cases wasted time and brought frustration. However, I did finally learn what to do and how to do it, and I began to make money. I consulted for *Fortune* 500 companies, for small businesses, for start-up companies, and for the government, and this endeavor continues to this day.

Then some years ago, within a few months of each other, I received my PhD and became a full-time university professor. (I might interject here that becoming a successful business consultant in many specialties does not require a PhD, an MBA, or in fact any business degree at all. But more about that later.) In any case, becoming a business professor did not curtail my consulting activities. If anything, it intensified them.

At my university I noticed that many students had a tremendous interest in business consulting—and not just business students. I was persuaded to develop an interdisciplinary course at California State University at Los Angeles on the subject of consulting for business. As this course developed, we did not stop at theory; every quarter I invited practicing consultants from many fields to share their experiences. These speakers ranged from small, one-person operations to staff consultants employed by multimillion-dollar corporations. My speakers included both full- and part-time consultants, and both men and women.

So popular did this course become that it attracted not only business students from all disciplines, but also psychologists, chemists, anthropologists, attorneys, and English majors. Many of those who took the course were older students from outside the university, including engineers, pilots, and many company executives and professionals who wanted to leave their corporate jobs, or to consult part-time. We even attracted a number of professors, who sat in on these lectures at various times to pick up what they could.

Partially due to the success of the business consulting course, another program for which I had responsibility also prospered. This was the Small Business Institute at the university, of which I was the director. The Small Business Institute program, conducted at universities around the country under the sponsorship of the U.S. Small Business Administration, furnishes consulting services to small businesses. The consulting is done by business students, supervised by professors. Over a period of years, we developed one of the largest Small Business Institutes in the country, and several times won district and regional awards for the top performance among participating universities. The Small Business Institute program allowed students in the consulting course to do hands-on projects as a part of their education.

Soon we had many requests for help from outside the university. In order to make this program mobile, we developed a consulting seminar that I have given at major universities several times a year over the last three years. These seminars were attended not only by neophyte and would-be consultants, but also by many consultants with considerable experience in their various professions. They generously shared their experiences and knowledge with other seminar students, and with me.

As a result, this book is based not only on my own experience, but also on that of many others, including numerous guest lecturers, professors, and students who have accomplished nearly 200 different consulting engagements for as many different small businesses, and the face-to-face interchange of ideas from consultants in many different fields and from many different geographical locations.

Had I had this book in my hands when I first started out, I would have saved myself thousands of wasted hours and much frustration. I would have avoided countless blunders, including journeys down blind alleys, while I struggled to learn how to promote my practice, develop long-term client relationships, and, in one case, get paid for services already performed.

This book contains the collective experiences of hundreds who have endeavored to earn their livelihood through the practice, either full- or part-time, of business consulting. Its aim is to help you to build a successful, rewarding business consultancy.

COHEN'S MAXIMS

· *Risk*. Never be afraid to take risks. If you work for someone, that is part of what you are getting paid for. If you work for yourself, it is the only way you can become successful.

· *Responsibility*. If you are assigned a task, you are responsible for its successful completion. There are no acceptable excuses for failing to fulfill this responsibility, and the responsibility cannot be shifted to others.

· *Self-Confidence*. Self-confidence comes from successfully completing increasingly difficult tasks and assignments. Give your maximum to every project, no matter how insignificant or formidable.

· *Leadership*. A leader accepts responsibility. This means that the welfare of those that you lead must always come before your own well-being. Therefore, while your primary duty is the accomplishment of your organization's mission, the welfare of your subordinates comes second, and your own welfare last.

· *Success*. Success does not come from working hard. Success comes from playing hard. Therefore, if you want success, you must position yourself so that the duties that you perform, no matter how difficult or challenging, are considered play to you and not work. If you do this, not only will you gain success, but you will have fun doing it.

· *Compensation*. Compensation, whether in the form of profit, salary, or job satisfaction, is the by-product of your contribution to society and is in direct proportion to this contribution. It is an error to make compensation the focus of your life's work. You will not reach your full potential, and you will have cheated society of the full benefit of your talent and ability.

· *Individual Ability*. Every individual has the potential to do great things. To reach this potential it is necessary to discover your special abilities and qualifications. This means that you should always attempt new tasks and accept responsibility for untried assignments whenever they are offered.

· *Duty*. Whatever your occupation, you have a duty to the society of which you are a member. If you are a soldier, your duty is to protect that society. If you are in business or industry, your duty is to create and manage the jobs, wealth, and products of that society. Therefore, failure will be harmful not only to you, but also to society, just as success will be beneficial not only to you, but also to society.

· *Planning*. Successful actions are not results of accidents or luck, but rather of an analysis of the situation and the preparation and proper execution of plans. Because of a changing environment and other variables, plans will not always succeed as originally conceived. But planning will maximize your successes and minimize your failures.

CONTENTS

Chapter 9   The Importance of Ethics in Consulting   86

Business Ethics Are Not Always Clear-Cut
    Ethics versus Jobs: The Lockheed Case☐The Ethics of Marketing
    Research☐An Executive Recruiting Story☐A Japanese View of
    Duty☐General Electric, Westinghouse, and Allis-Chambers
Typical Problems of Ethics in Consulting

Chapter 10   Making Professional Presentations   97

Objectives of Presentations☐Five Keys to a Successful Presentation
    Professionalism☐Enthusiasm☐Organization☐Practice
        Controlling Time☐The Practice Sequence☐The Formal Practice
        Presentation☐Live Demonstration
    Visual Aids
        Flip Charts☐Overhead Transparencies☐35mm Slides☐Handouts
Overcoming Stage Fright☐Answering Questions

Chapter 11   How to Run Your Consulting Business   109

Selecting the Legal Structure for Your Consulting Firm
    The Sole Proprietorship
        Advantages☐Disadvantages
    The Partnership
        How a Partnership Differs from a Sole
        Proprietorship☐Advantages☐Disadvantages
    The Corporation
        Advantages☐Disadvantages
Other Legal Necessities
    Obtaining a Business License☐The Resale Permit☐Fictitious Name
    Registration
Clients' Use of Credit Cards☐Stationery and Business
Cards☐Insurance and Personal Liability
    Insurance Checklist
Keeping Overhead Low
    The Telephone☐Anticipating Expenses
Necessary Records and Their Maintenance☐Tax Obligations
    Income Taxes☐Withholding Income Taxes☐Withholding Social
    Security Taxes☐Remitting Federal Taxes☐Excise
    Taxes☐Unemployment Taxes☐Obtaining an Employer
    Identification Number☐State and Local Taxes☐Minimizing Tax
    Paperwork

1
THE INCREDIBLE BUSINESS OF CONSULTING

Consulting has to be one of the most incredible businesses around, with advantages possessed by no other way of making a living. Consider working hours. You probably have some time of the day when you work best. Most people do. Some people work better in the morning, others in the evening, and a very few people work equally well all day. But in consulting, it doesn't make any difference, because you pick your own hours. *You* decide when you work and when you do not. You can always work at your best time.

Are you in a job where you don't like your boss? Must you work with people that you just do not care to be around? Well, in consulting, you decide whom you wish to work for and whom you do not wish to work for, as well as whom you do and do not work with. Whether you do or do not work for a particular client is entirely up to you.

Are you dissatisfied with your current salary? In consulting, you set your own fees; *you* decide how much you're worth and how much you want to make. If you are worth more right now, today, you can give yourself a raise.

Do you prefer to work at home? In consulting, you can make $100,000 or more working out of your own home without worrying about parking, driving, or the expense of an outside office. In fact, the office in your own home is tax-deductible.

Finally, are you concerned with making the big plunge of going into your own full-time consulting practice? No need to risk this. You can actually start in consulting part-time and ease your way in. Many successful consultants have started through part-time work after their full-time jobs, at nights and on weekends. And if you follow the instructions in this book, you will soon be able to build a successful consulting practice, and you will not have to quit your full-time job until you are fully ready and certain that you will be successful.

WHAT IS CONSULTING?

Consultants operate in many, many different fields. Import-export, management, engineering, and marketing are some of the common ones.

There are consultants in archaeology and clothes selection. There are even consultants to help authors overcome writer's block. In my classes and in seminars around the country, I have met experts from all those fields, and more. All had become or had the potential for becoming successful consultants. In fact, my *Los Angeles Times* this morning (January 20, 1984) contained the story of an enormously successful consulting business run by a young mother. She worked about six days every month, advising businesses which records to keep and which to throw away.

A consultant is simply anyone who gives advice or performs other services of a professional or semiprofessional nature, in return for compensation. This means that regardless of your area of interest or expertise, you can become a consultant. Everyone has a unique background, with special experiences and interests duplicated by few others, and in demand by certain individuals or companies at certain times.

Many of my students ask whether it is necessary to have an advanced degree in order to be a consultant. The answer is definitely no. Although the orientation of a consultant is clearly professional, I have known many successful consultants with limited formal academic training. The important thing is that you have the necessary experience, qualifications, and skills to help with a task that an individual or company wants performed. Where you obtained these skills is of far less importance. Now, I do want to add that if it is your intent to work as a management consultant for a major consulting firm and not on your own, this is not true. Here an MBA will probably be required. But if you are on your own, whether or not you obtained your expertise from a university is not crucial. I know of a successful import-export consultant with no degree, and a $700-a-day consultant to top management of major corporations who has no MBA, only an undergraduate degree in sociology.

HOW BIG IS THE CONSULTING INDUSTRY?

Because consulting encompasses so many different aspects of life, it is very difficult to measure precisely the total dollar volume for consulting services currently performed in the United States. Most people are able only to estimate the value of consulting services being performed for business. Current estimates for business consulting are between $2.5 and $3 billion per year, and growing at 20% every single year.

Consulting for Business

Even business consulting encompasses a very, very wide area of activities. Jerome Fuchs, author of *Making the Most of Management Consulting*

Services (New York: AMACOM, 1975), categorized consulting activities into eleven different areas.

1. General management, encompassing organizational planning, strategy, and other general management tasks.
2. Manufacturing, including production control, facilities management, and so forth.
3. Personnel, having to do with development and training, recruitment, selection, management of employee benefits programs, and other similar activities.
4. Marketing, covering such topics as new product introduction, pricing, promotion, and development of distribution channels.
5. Finance and accounting, including cost accounting, valuation, tax advice, investment programs, and so forth.
6. Procurement and purchasing.
7. Research and development, and potential product selection and screening.
8. Packaging, including aspects such as packaging machinery, design, and testing.
9. Administration, including office management and administrative procedures.
10. International operations, which has to do with import, export, licensing, tariffs, and joint ventures.
11. Specialized services, which catches all the many other areas, such as executive recruiting, telecommunications, and the like.

Consultants News, a newsletter of the consulting industry, surveyed 583 firms to find out what type of consulting expertise they offered. (Appendix A contains an address for *Consultants News* as well as a list of other references helpful to consultants.) Here are the results:

Consulting Expertise Offered	*Number of Firms Offering*
General Management	219
Personnel	143
Marketing	126
Organizational Planning	113
Manufacturing	112
Management Development	100
Strategic Business Planning	97
Administration	96

Finance and Accounting   89
Marketing Strategy and Organization   82

You might be interested to know that there are several associations that certify management consulting companies or individual management consultants. They are: the Association of Consulting Management Engineers (230 Park Avenue, New York, NY 10017, 212–697–9693); the Association of Management Consultants (500 N. Michigan Avenue, Suite 1400, Chicago, IL 60611, 312–266–1261); the Institute of Management Consultants (19 West 44th Street, New York, NY 10036, 212–921–2885); and the Society of Professional Management Consultants (16 West 56th Street, New York, NY 10019, 212–586–2041).

Types of Consulting Firms

Consulting firms may also be defined by other aspects of their business, including size, location, and the type of client they serve. This means you can speak about:

1. *National general management firms.* These are large firms such as McKinsey and Company, Booz-Allen, or Arthur D. Little, which do millions and millions of dollars in consulting business every single year.
2. *Major accounting firms with consulting divisions.* Most national CPA firms today, including all of the Big Eight, have divisions that do management consulting in addition to their regular accounting activities.
3. *Functionally specialized firms.* These organizations specialize in certain particular areas of business. Such a firm might deal only in market research, or strategic planning.
4. *Industry-specific firms.* These are large national or international firms dealing only with certain industries or certain types of operations. An example would be Theodore Barry, International, which was once known primarily for its work in the utility industry.
5. *Public sector firms.* These firms specialize in consulting primarily with the government, either national, state, or local, or for nonprofit organizations such as universities or hospitals.
6. *The so-called think tanks.* These very large firms, such as Rand and SRI International, may have many or very few customers. The Aerospace Corporation, located in Los Angeles, deals mainly with the U.S. Air Force.

7. *Regional and local firms.* There are numerous consulting firms that operate in a single geographic area, even though their annual sales may be quite large.
8. *Sole practitioners.* This is an area many new consultants seek, and well they might. There are currently between 35,000 and 50,000 such consulting businesses in America; more than half of these are one-person operations, and another 20%–25% have between two and ten people.
9. *Specialty firms outside of business.* This may actually be one of the largest areas of consulting, although it is rarely counted because the focus is outside the area of business. Such firms may consult on health, etiquette, dress, or even personal behavioral management.

This wide variety indicates that the opportunities in the consulting business are tremendous. Many of the local or regional firms, and even the larger firms, started small with a sole practitioner and grew to be multi-million-dollar giants.

WHY DOES ANYONE NEED A CONSULTANT ANYWAY?

You may ask yourself why it is that a large business firm hires a consultant, at sometimes very, very high compensation, when it already has staffs of experts who, one would think, should be even more qualified than the consultant. In a television broadcast several years ago, *60 Minutes* asked this very question about consultants to the government. After all, if the government employees themselves are qualified, why the need to hire consultants? And why pay them more than the employees themselves are being paid?

Actually, there are very good reasons why both the government and business organizations use consultants. In fact, not only are they hired, they are hired again and again and held in considerable esteem. Because it is good business to find a need and then fill it, it is very important for you to understand exactly what these reasons are. Let's look at each of them in turn.

1. *Lack of available personnel.* Sometimes even the largest firms lack personnel at specific periods of time or for specific tasks. They may need assistance during a temporary work overload, or they may require unique expertise that is not needed on an ongoing basis every day of the year. Temporary assistance might be needed, for example, when a firm bids for a government contract. During this period, it is required to put out a great

amount of work over a short period of time. The staff personnel may not be available to do this without stopping other important projects, so consultants are hired. Or a firm may need unique expertise on a short-term, project basis. Take direct marketing, an area I frequently consult in. Many firms use direct marketing only occasionally, so it does not make sense to hire a full-time expert whose salary could easily exceed $50,000 per year. Therefore, a company is perfectly happy to hire a consultant, at fees of from $50 to $300 an hour, to accomplish a specific task.

2. *The need for an outside opinion.* Not infrequently a company has a problem and management feels the employees are too close to it to understand all the ramifications. It makes sense then to bring in someone from outside—someone with competent problem-solving skills but not necessarily knowledge of the business. In fact, sometimes the individual's very ignorance (assuming, of course, a talent for problem-solving) helps to provide the answer. Peter F. Drucker, perhaps the world's greatest and certainly the most famous management consultant, has frequently said that he brings to the problem not so much his experience in a specific industry as his ignorance. He has a tremendous ability to penetrate through a confusion of factors and recognize the main issue, and thus to make recommendations that will enable the problem to be solved. This makes his services well worth the fees he charges.

3. *Company politics.* At times the solution to a problem may actually be known, but for various political reasons it cannot be presented by those who understand the problem. For example, a division of a major company once proposed that the company enter a new market with one of its products, which would have required an investment of millions of dollars. Because the new product would come from the division that suggested it, the division's recommendations could be considered prejudiced. However, by hiring an outside consultant to study the same issues, the division succeeded in accomplishing the same thing. The consultant was assumed to be more impartial and less likely to be influenced by company politics.

4. *A need for improved sales.* No company can exist without sales. This is true no matter how knowledgeable its president or senior staff, how skilled its financial people and accountants, how innovative its engineers in developing or manufacturing new products. A company that needs to increase sales rapidly will sometimes turn outside its own marketing staff for help.

5. *The need for capital.* Every company needs money. This is especially true of a successful company. In fact, the more successful a company, the more capital it needs. The need for capital is a continuing problem with many companies. An individual who has expertise in finding sources of capital will be in continual demand.

6. *Government regulations*. Government regulations, if not obeyed, can result in fines, imprisonment, or even the closing down of the business. No company is immune to government regulations, and all companies need to ensure that they fulfill these regulations in the most efficient and effective manner. At the same time they wish to minimize any negative impact on their business and, if possible, use the regulations to help the operation of their business. These regulations concern many areas: equal employment opportunity, age discrimination, consumer credit protection, safety standards, veterans' rights, and numerous others. If you have knowledge in any of these regulatory areas or can become an expert in them, there is a real market for your consulting services.

7. *The need for maximum efficiency*. All organizations need to operate in as efficient a manner as possible. An organization that operates at lower efficiency than it is capable of will eventually have problems. Other, more efficient competitors will take away its market and drive it out of business. Inefficiency will lead to high costs, making prices uncompetitive. Slippages, delays, and low productivity all result from inefficiency. If you know how to increase the efficiency of an organization, you have something important to sell as a consultant.

8. *The ability to diagnose problems and find solutions*. One reason that the MBA degree (Master of Business Administration) is so sought after by many businesses is that the graduates with these degrees are supposed to be very adept at diagnosing problems faced by business and developing solutions for them. Anyone who can do this is in demand. The more general problem-solving you do and the better you become at it, the more your name will get around. Large consulting firms have capitalized on the need of businesses to have their problems diagnosed and recommendations for solutions made. For this reason, these firms have sought to hire MBAs from the top schools at extremely high starting salaries in order to build and maintain a reputation for problem-solving. Even some individual practitioners such as Peter F. Drucker are nationally and sometimes internationally known for their problem-solving talents.

9. *Training employees*. The operation of any business is becoming more and more complex, and today many employees are continually trained throughout their careers. Managers need different types of training for leadership, organizational, and planning skills; computer operators need additional training with the latest equipment, techniques, software, and programming. In fact, developments are occurring so rapidly that virtually every single functional area of business needs continual training. If you are an expert and can remain up to date in any area that is in demand, you have a niche in a type of consulting that commands large fees from industry.

Remember, these are the reasons that businesses normally need consultants. There are also thousands of other areas in which both business and nonbusiness people may need assistance. For example, consultants are making millions of dollars today by teaching people how to manage their time, control stress, lose weight, and keep fit. If you have specific knowledge in almost any area—from handicrafts to hypnotism, mathematics to merchandising—you may have skills that are in demand by some segment of the population.

WHAT MAKES AN OUTSTANDING CONSULTANT?

Being a consultant and being an outstanding consultant are two different things. After talking with many top-flight consultants around the country, I have identified seven areas that make the difference.

1. *Bedside manner.* This refers to your ability to get along with your client. Here it's not so much what you say, but how you say it. Doctors with much knowledge but poor bedside manner often find that their patients prefer to go to doctors with much less experience or ability. Developing a pleasant bedside manner, so that your clients have confidence in what you say, can be as important as your technical knowledge.

2. *The ability to diagnose problems.* To stay with the doctor analogy, we know that the doctor has access to all sorts of medicines to help cure a patient. But if he or she makes an incorrect diagnosis, the medicine may hurt more than it helps. Similarly, your ability to diagnose the problem correctly is extremely important. It is one of the most significant criteria of an outstanding consultant.

3. *The ability to find solutions.* Of course, having once diagnosed a problem, now you are expected to recommend the proper actions to correct the situation. You will find an entire chapter in this book devoted to problem-solving. With practice, you will be able to solve complex problems consistently by suggesting the right course of action for your client to take.

4. *Technical expertise and knowledge.* Perhaps you expected this would be the most important skill for a good consultant, and it is true that technical expertise in a field is important. Expertise comes from your education, your experience, and the personal skills you have developed. But it may be in any one of a variety of areas and it may develop in a variety of different ways. G. Gordon Liddy, known primarily for his association with the Watergate break-in, today commands a six-figure income as a security consultant. Note that even a background that includes incarceration in a

penitentiary does not affect your ability to be a good consultant and to make a major contribution to the benefit of your client.

5. *Communication skills.* Charles Garvin, from the well-known Boston Consulting Group, has done extensive consulting in the area of business strategy since the early 1960s. From more than 20 years' experience, Garvin has identified three major attributes that every good consultant needs. He believes the number one attribute is superior communication abilities. (Analytical skill is second, and the ability to work under pressure is third.)

Some years ago a study of how companies viewed recent business school graduates was conducted by Dr. Allen Blitstein. Dr. Blitstein wanted to know two things: the most important factors in why new graduates were hired, and the major factors that indicated success on the job after hiring. You may have thought that such factors as grade point average or perhaps the school attended would be of primary importance. But not so. According to the employers who did the hiring, the most important factors had to do with the ability to communicate. And that was true both for getting hired and for success on the job. You should study the chapter on presentations with particular interest.

6. *Marketing and selling ability.* Regardless of the technical area you are interested in, whether it is a functional area in business or something entirely different, you must learn to be a good marketer and a good salesperson. For consultants sell not only an intangible product, they also must sell themselves. There is a special chapter on marketing your business and yourself; every secret I have learned from my own experiences or from other consultants, I have revealed to you.

7. *Management skills.* Last, but not the least in importance, is the ability to manage a business or a practice and to run projects. In my mind, an outstanding consultant must also be a good manager. As with other skills, the ability to manage can be learned. To assist you in this process, there's a special chapter on managing your business efficiently. In addition, throughout the book I give step-by-step instructions for many processes that will help you perform as a skilled manager.

Dick Brodkorb is the president and founder of a consulting company in Costa Mesa, California, called Decision Planning, Inc. Dick frequently speaks to my classes in consulting. He has identified two groups of skills that he feels are most important in making a good consultant. He calls them "The Big Three" and "The Big Four." The Big Three are communication skills, both written and oral; technical command of a subject; and the ability to get along with others.

He suggests that neophyte consultants first master The Big Three, and then move on to The Big Four. The first is analytical skills (not necessarily quantitative). Second, Dick says sensitivity to others is extremely important. Third, the consultant should have a tolerance for the consulting lifestyle, which may require intensive hours of work on some projects. Finally, Dick says that a consultant needs to have a strong personal drive to be successful.

In summary, there are certain things you must know in order to be a consultant. These are:

- How to become expert in your field
- How to get clients
- How to diagnose and solve problems
- How to run your practice

All these topics, and a lot more, are covered in this book.

It's important to recognize that you may not need actual hands-on experience in your technical area of interest at first. One of my MBA students went to work for one of the largest consulting firms in the country with no hands-on experience at all, using solely what he had learned as a student. Peter F. Drucker once said that although he consults internationally for major corporations, he has never been a practicing manager with the single exception of serving as dean at Bennington School for approximately two years in the 1940s.

HOW MUCH MONEY CAN YOU MAKE AS A CONSULTANT?

No one should embark on a career as a consultant primarily to make money. Still, money is needed to live, and it can provide the freedom to choose what one wishes to do in life and for whom. So, this is a valid question, and I will attempt to answer it to the best of my ability.

Several years ago Professor Laurie Laurwood of Claremont Graduate School surveyed 150 California consulting firms, both sole practitioners and major firms. She found that the average firm did $250,000 a year in business. Other surveys of sole practitioners at about the same time indicated that a typical first year's gross for a consultant ranged from $20,000 to $40,000, and that the average consultant billed at between $300 and $600 a day.

I am going to discuss pricing your services in detail in a later chapter, but for now, when you are considering the potential of the business, it is important to realize that you will not be able to bill for every minute of every day. Some time must be spent in marketing your services. Therefore, it's important to consider the ratio of billable time to time spent marketing, which is not billable. Howard L. Shenson, who has given seminars around the country on consulting, told me once that he estimates new consultants should plan to spend at least one third of their time the first year marketing their services, and only two thirds in actual billable time. After the first year, marketing time can be reduced to 15% or 20%. Other estimates for marketing time have ranged as high as 40%–50%. Many independent consultants note that, once established, they spend almost no time marketing, since they receive additional clients through referrals or spend all their available time on established clients.

When estimating how much you can actually make as a consultant, it is better to start with the assumption that the first year you will spend about one half of your time marketing your services. You may not actually need that much, but it's safer than expecting to spend most of your time on work billed to your clients and then finding that you have grossly overestimated your first year's sales.

HOW DO PEOPLE BECOME CONSULTANTS?

Individuals get into consulting through many strange ways, and no two stories are exactly alike. You may be interested in hearing how some consultants got their start.

Howard L. Shenson was a PhD student at the same time that he was teaching and serving as department head at California State University at Northridge. He received numerous requests from companies in the local area, and he soon was engaged in a variety of consulting activities in addition to his teaching and research. As the months went by he realized he was spending more and more time consulting, and finding it more fascinating than his academic work. Finally he decided to devote himself entirely to full-time consulting, and found not only better job satisfaction but far greater compensation than he could ever earn as a professor.

Hubert Bermont, author of the self-published *How to Become a Successful Consultant in Your Own Field* and a successful consultant in the publishing industry as well as a consultant's consultant today, got his start when his boss called him in one day and fired him. Bermont said he went through total shock at the time, but later realized it was a favor in disguise. In desperation, Bermont called around and found a friend who agreed to let him use his office, secretary, and telephone for a nominal sum in exchange for training his friend's new secretary. He was able to attain as a client the most prestigious and successful name in his business by working for the company at the right price—nothing. This door-opener eventually led to a paying contract with the firm and, more important, gave him a major client with which to impress other prospective clients. At the end of six months, he was earning almost as much as it had taken him 20 years to reach in his previous career.

Phil Ross started out as an actor who worked as a salesman with a manufacturing company between jobs. Because of his unique abilities not only to sell, but also to educate and motivate, he soon became national sales director. When he became dissatisfied with company policies, he began looking for another job, using a national executive search firm. In the process, he was recruited by that firm to become an executive recruiter, or "headhunter." Search consulting probably calls for more sales skills than any other type of consulting, since the consultant must be able to convince a firm to become a client *and* persuade a fully satisfied employee to consider leaving his or her present firm and become a candidate for a job with a different company. Phil mastered these skills and excelled as a search consultant, and soon he was appointed national training director. After several years, Phil left to start his own executive search firm and eventually founded THE PROS, a consulting company that assists corporations worldwide with their personnel and recruitment problems.

Luis Espinosa was born in Mexico and was my student at California State University at Los Angeles. He wanted to become a consultant for a major consulting firm. Using special job-finding techniques that got him face-to-face interviews with principals of top consulting firms, he was soon hired by Theodore Barry, International. After only two years, he was recruited as a top-level strategic planner for a bank in Mexico City with $20 billion in assets. He then went on to a similar high position as an internal strategic planning consultant with an American bank.

This points out yet another advantage of consulting. Not infrequently, consultants who are highly visible to top management so impress their clients with their performance that they are catapulted immediately into senior executive ranks at extremely high salaries. Several years ago *Business Week* carried the story of Ilene Gordon Bluestein, who became director of corporate planning at the Signode Corporation in Glenview, Illionis, at age 28, only four years after graduating from college. The point here is that those four years were spent in consulting. Bluestein wasn't the only success mentioned. This article told of other women who used consulting as a springboard to corporate success. All were young, held senior positions, and made large salaries. And every single one had been a consultant.

In this chapter we've had an overview of the entire consulting business, and I hope I've opened your eyes to some of the potentials, both in the lifestyle of a consultant and in the compensation you might receive, as well as different consulting areas that you might enjoy. Finally, although I've mentioned stories of several individuals who have become consultants, I think it's important for you to realize that it is not so important *how* you become a consultant, as that you actually *become* one. There are many routes to becoming a consultant, but the bottom line—success as a consultant—is what counts. This process will start in the next chapter, with your learning how to get clients.

2
HOW TO GET CLIENTS

This chapter discusses one of the most important aspects of any consulting business—getting clients. Without clients, there can be no business. No matter how expert the consultant and no matter what the field, without clients the business and the practice cannot exist. In this chapter you will find not only conventional methods of marketing your practice and obtaining clients, but also some ways that may not be so obvious. I call these "indirect methods" of marketing your services. Although they take longer, they can greatly expand your practice. To build a dynamic practice, you should integrate both direct and indirect methods into your marketing program.

DIRECT METHODS OF MARKETING

With the six direct methods of marketing listed as follows, you approach potential clients directly and let them know that you are available:

1. Direct mail
2. Cold calls
3. Direct response advertising
4. Directory listings
5. Yellow Pages listings
6. Former employers

Let's look at each in turn.

Direct Mail

With direct mail you send potential clients a letter, or a brochure, or both, advertising your services. An example of a page from a catalog used in direct mail is shown in Figure 2–1. It is very similar to a direct mail letter. Note that it talks directly to the client's needs and tries to avoid sounding pompous or distant. The writer is attempting to establish direct communication with the potential client. By suggesting accomplishments of the firm in the past, the writer implies the kinds of things that can be done for this new client in the future. Finally, the piece doesn't leave things

Figure 2-1. Example of an effective direct mail piece.

AN OVERVIEW OF
SALES AND MARKETING CONSULTING
WITH STEVEN WEST AND HIS GROUP

There are many occasions in which the complexity or importance of a problem or a situation mandates the use of an outside consultant.

Outside consultants maintain a detached objectivity. They don't get emotionally involved in the internal politics or fixed way of thinking of the past. Consultants bring with them fresh ideas. They are emissaries of new information. Often, they will cross-pollinate ideas between clients and act as a conduit for new technology. Consultants bring with them specialized talent. This highly specialized talent can be hired to solve a particular problem, define a particular opportunity and then that assignment can be completed. Consultants become part-time, pro tempore members of your staff. They give you depth and allow you to maintain a lean and mean payroll. And consultants will often work on a fixed fee basis, so that you know exactly what your costs will be. There are no guesses and no equivocation.

Steven West and the New York Marketing Group are considered to be the world's leading sales and marketing consultants. Their 7 operating divisions can bring sharpness of focus and expertise to bear upon unique and complex problems at your company. They combine a no-nonsense, real life experience with the most sophisticated cutting edge technology. Their unique blending of pragmatic, straight-line thinking, coupled with advanced strategies and tactics in sales and marketing, are fitted to your company's needs to find solutions to problems. But their solutions are focused on reality —not in graphs-charts-philosophies-models.

New York Marketing Group and its affiliates are the largest private sales and marketing consulting company in the world. More than 50 specialists each focus in on specific areas of sales and marketing consultation. Under the direction and leadership of Steven West, this group can marshal its resources to assist you in solving your unique corporate problems.

More than 1/8 of the Fortune 500 companies and half of America's largest banks utilize Steven West and his associates to help solve their unique consulting problems. Companies such as Revlon, Sears, Wang, Citicorp, Manufacturers Hanover, Data General, GTE, Nynex Telephone Company and Bell South are just a few of the clients who utilize Steven West's services.

Many smaller companies whose names, no doubt, would mean nothing to you, are active users of Steven West and his company's services. You need not be a multi-billion dollar, multi-national company to take advantage of the expertise of this group.

Fees, seniority and experience level can be adjusted to suit your respective budgets. This group can readily undertake projects in the millions of dollars. Conversely, projects of a few thousand dollars are welcome with the same level of enthusiasm.

Whether your requirements are for a few days of consultation, or an in-depth, on-going relationship, Steven West and his associates will be happy to explore working with your company.

A Word of Caution—The New York Marketing Group and Steven West will not accept any assignments that they feel would not be fruitful for their clients. If what you have in mind is not going to work, or if there is a probability that it is unlikely to work, your project will not be accepted.

Recently, a top executive at Baush & Lomb said, "In talking to my friends in the business community, what sets aside Steven West and his group from all other sales and marketing consultants, is their batting average. 96% of the time they will find the solution that you are looking for. If they don't think that you are barking up the right tree, they'll politely reject the assignment." This is professionalism in its ultimate development. For information call:

(718) 479-3700

There are 7 specialized areas of consultion in which you can utilize Steven West and his group.

THE NEW YORK MARKETING GROUP
61-47 188th Street
Fresh Meadows, NY 11365

Courtesy of The New York Marketing Group.

hanging; at the very end, the prospective client is asked to call at once for additional information or to set up a consulting appointment.

The basic purpose of any brochure is, first, to advertise your type of work and, second, to convince the reader that you are the most capable individual available to do this work. Therefore, if you are going to develop your own brochure, write it to answer the two questions, "What is it that I do?" and "Why am I the best?" Answering these questions may require that your brochure have different sections. Such sections might include descriptions of the kind of work you do; specific examples of problems you have solved for clients in the past, along with benefits they have accrued from using your services; reasons why your services are better than those offered by competitors; your experience, background, and special qualifications that make you unique; a list of previous clients (if available); and perhaps even some testimonials from previous clients. If you haven't done any consulting previously, you can write down accomplishments that you attained when you were an employee. As long as these accomplishments were in your area of consulting expertise and benefited whomever you were working for at the time, it is unimportant whether the beneficiary was an employer or a client. There are a number of good books available to help you in preparing your own brochure. One of the best is *How to Prepare Professional Design Brochures* by Gerre Jones (New York: McGraw-Hill, 1976).

Your brochure should be accompanied by your direct mail letter. The format of your brochure could be anything from a simple one-page flier, to a slick, many-paged booklet, or something in between. Small consulting operations often get good results with a modest brochure, perhaps one 8½" × 11" sheet folded twice, which describes the background of the company, the type of work it does, and the qualifications of the principal or principals. Many of the very large firms produce quite elaborate brochures, covering all aspects of the practice, which are designed to impress clients with the stature, size, and accomplishments of the firm simply by the brochure itself.

Sample pages from an excellent brochure, which falls somewhere in between, are found in Appendix B. Mickey Rosenau, owner of the Rosenau Consulting Company of Santa Monica, California, has divided his brochure into different topic headings such as Company, What We Do, Clients, Qualifications, Recent Assignments, Our Code of Professional Responsibility, Contractual Terms and Conditions, Case Histories, How We Work, Why Retain the Rosenau Consulting Company, and Client Relationships. A brochure like this goes a long way toward making a sale even before the consultant meets the potential client face to face for the first time.

Locating the Right Mailing List

Producing your letter, brochure, and its first-class envelope is not inexpensive. You can expect to spend as much as 50¢ or more including postage to get each direct mail package to a potential client. Therefore, you do not want to waste your mailing on individuals who have but slight chance of being interested in your services. You want to reach those who are real potential customers—individuals who have the authority to hire you and would probably be interested in what you have to offer.

One source of help are those professionals who handle mailing lists: list brokers, managers, or compilers. These experts can be found in most Yellow Pages under the heading "Mailing Lists." They will discuss your needs with you and help you rent lists of potential clients interested in the particular services you offer. Usually you will pay nothing for this advice on lists. The list broker gets paid a commission from the list owner when you rent the lists.

If you are located in a smaller town, the potential size of your market, depending upon your specialty, may be so small that a direct mail campaign may not be advisable. On the other hand, you could do a direct mail campaign with the idea of promoting a national or international business. This, of course, may require travel on your part, unless you consult through the mail or by telephone, both of which are possible.

One firm that successfully promotes its business through the mail is the MTA Group Management and Technology Advisers, Inc., a small consulting firm involved in production for the publishing industry. It has spent as much as $45,000 a year on its direct mail campaign alone. The company also uses this method to stay in touch with its client list of about 6,000 companies by mailing out to them up to six different first-class packages (each containing a letter, a card, and a small brochure) and then sending the same mailings out a second time, all within the span of a year. From this, MTA Group Management and Technology Advisers, Inc. gets a gross response of about 1.8%, according to *Direct Marketing News* of November 15, 1983.

If you would like to receive additional information or catalogs of lists, contact the following:

Ed Burnett Consultants, Inc.
2 Park Ave., New York, N.Y. 10016
212-679-0630   Toll free 800-223-7777

Cahners Publishing Company
1350 E. Touhy Ave., Des Plaines, Ill. 60018
312-635-8800

Dunhill International List, Inc.
2430 W. Oakland Park Blvd., Ft. Lauderdale, Fla. 33311
800-223-1882 (toll free)

Dun's Marketing Services, a company of the Dun &
Bradstreet Corporation
3 Century Dr., Parsippany, N.J. 07054
800-526-9018 (toll free)

National Business Lists, Inc.
162 N. Franklin St., Chicago, Ill. 60606
312-236-0350   Toll free 800-621-6487

Fred Woolf List Co., Inc.
280 N. Central Ave., Hartsdale, N.Y. 10530
914-946-0336   212-679-4311   Toll free 800-431-1557

Alvin B. Zeller, Inc.
475 Park Ave. South, New York, N.Y. 10016
212-689-4900   Toll free 800-223-0814

Zeller & Letica, Inc.
15 E. 26 St., New York, N.Y. 10010
212-685-6278   Toll free 800-221-4112

Advanced Management Systems, Inc.
9255 Sunset Blvd., Penthouse, Los Angeles, Calif. 90069
213-858-1520

Market Compilation & Research Bureau, Inc. (MCRB)
230 Park Ave., Suite 2725, New York, N.Y. 10169
212-661-1250

Hank Marshall Marketing
P.O. Box 2729, Laguna Hills, Calif. 92653
714-581-5856

Cold Calls

Cold calls are those made to prospects with whom you have had no
prior contact. This method can be extremely effective in obtaining clients.
However, it is time-consuming, and it involves significant rejection, which
you must learn to cope with if you are to use this method.

Let's say you decided to devote a single day to obtaining clients
through cold calls. That means you should make 25–30 actual contacts
with individuals who have the authority to hire you. If even half this num-

ber retained your services, you would soon be extremely wealthy from consulting. As a matter of fact, you would have more consulting work than you could possibly handle. But the reality is that if one of these calls leads to a one-time engagement of $3,000–$5,000, the day was well worth your time. If you consider that this is a satisfied client who will hire you again and again, this single success out of many calls was really worthwhile. However, 25–30 calls with one success mean 24–29 rejections, some of which will be rude and abrupt. Therefore, if you wish to use cold-calling, you must train yourself to be prepared for the rejection that accompanies its use.

You can maximize your success in using the cold-call method by doing the following:

1. *Write out exactly what you want to say ahead of time.* Usually you should follow the outline of a good direct mail letter. That is, you should speak about benefits to your potential client and sell yourself by describing past accomplishments. (These could be things you did while employed full-time for someone else. The important thing is that you were the one responsible and actually did whatever it is you have claimed.) While planning what you are going to say, never forget that the object is *not* to make a sale over the phone, which is almost impossible to accomplish. Rather, your goal should be to get a face-to-face interview where you can close the sale. (I'll show you how to do that in the next chapter.) So now you know how to tell a successful cold call: it always ends with an appointment for a face-to-face interview.

2. *Use creative ways to get around the secretary.* One of the most bothersome aspects about the cold-call method is that frequently executives who may wish to hire you have secretaries in place between you and them. Part of their job is to screen out job-seekers and those wanting to sell something to their bosses. Therefore, it is essential that you get through the secretary. One method is simply to avoid the secretary altogether—call before 8:00 A.M. or after 5:00 P.M., and chances are the manager will answer the call directly. Another technique is to identify yourself by name and ask for the individual you wish to speak with, using his or her full name. If you do not have this name, call the company and ask the receptionist for the individual's full name, not just Mr. Smith but Don Smith. The receptionist will connect you with the executive's secretary. Then you say, firmly, "This is Jim Black for Don Smith. Would you connect me please?" Or you can say, "This is Jim Black, president of the XYZ Consulting Group, for Don Smith. Would you connect me please?" If the secretary asks the nature of your call, say that it is a private business matter. If she refuses to connect you without having this information, ask her to forward the information to her boss and leave your number for him to call

you back. The chances of getting through are better this way than if you say that you are selling consulting services. Too many individuals have been there before you, and there is a good chance that the executive has told the secretary to screen all such calls.

3. *Combine your calls with a direct mail campaign.* This one-two combination punch can work very well. Do the direct mail campaign first, then wait several weeks. This gives the executive time to call you directly if she wishes, and you will have a greater chance of setting up an interview. After several weeks have gone by, you cold-call those who have not responded to your mailing. Now if the secretary asks the reason for the call, you can say that it has to do with a letter you wrote previously to Don Smith. If you're wondering whether to include in the letter a statement that you will call soon, my recommendation is no. For one thing, if you indicate that you will call, the executive who may otherwise have called may not do so, and it's always much better if she responds immediately rather than passively waiting for you to call. Second, if you get very busy, either with other aspects of your marketing campaign or with consulting work, your call will be delayed and you could lose a sale. The direct mail campaign, combined with a cold-call follow-up, works well because some executives who desperately need your services may not realize it from your letter. In a personal conversation, they may recognize that you can fulfill their need and will make an appointment for an interview.

Advertising

Until fairly recently, the advertising of consulting services was not particularly common. Today, it is done successfully for a number of different types of consultants. Executive search consultants, for instance, have advertised in magazines or trade journals in their areas of specialty. Since potential clients in certain industries prefer to deal with specialists, these ads have been successful. However, advertisements for other consulting services, including research consulting, have been less successful; some are even prohibited by their consulting associations. Consultants tend to be equated with attorneys and doctors, in terms of confidentiality and standards of professionalism; since only recently have the ethics codes of these two professions permitted advertising, it is no wonder that the same has been generally true for consulting.

However, depending upon the type of services you offer, some sort of advertising may be effective and acceptable. If you decide to advertise, it is important that the ad be well written, which means written with your potential clients in mind, and placed in a medium that they read.

Advertising is expensive. Further, learning how to write the copy that makes such advertising work is not easy. The type of advertising that you are interested in is direct response advertising. Like a direct mail letter or cold calling by telephone, this type of advertising is intended to bring a direct response. At the very least, such an ad should result in inquiries that will lead to consulting engagements. Even some professional writers cannot write this kind of copy. The copy must be so compelling that prospective clients needing your services would be foolish not to contact you. Most such advertisements use the AIDA formula—Attention, Interest, Desire, and Action. A dramatic headline is used to attract people's attention. Their interest is immediately aroused in the lead-in paragraphs through the statement of specific benefit. Additional benefits are stated and talked about until their desire to respond to the ad is at a peak. At this point, the ad calls upon them to respond at once by taking specific action.

If you want to advertise your services, I would recommend that you read the following books: *Building a Mail Order Business*, 2nd ed., by William A. Cohen (New York: John Wiley & Sons, Inc., 1985); *Tested Advertising Methods*, 4th ed., by John Caples (Englewood Cliffs, N.J.: Prentice-Hall, 1974); and *How to Write a Good Advertisement* by Victor O. Schwab (North Hollywood, Calif.: Wilshire Book Co., 1980).

Directory Listings

There are many directories that list consultants and the particular services they provide. Some are free; some charge for listings. Usually this method of advertising is not very effective for a simple reason: few potential clients use directories when seeking consultants. As a test, I once paid $300 to be listed in one of these directories. Over the period of a year, I received numerous letters about my listing, but every single one was from someone seeking to sell *me* something! Directory listings are not recommended for the average consultant unless they are free.

Yellow Pages Listings

Listings in the Yellow Pages of your telephone book may be effective for certain general types of consulting practices. Clients who have never used a consultant before, in particular, often turn to the Yellow Pages in search of such services. If you decide to advertise this way, it is important that you buy a large ad. The psychology of this is simple. A larger ad will attract potential clients over a competitor's smaller ad. Second, many people assume that a large ad is placed by a large company and a small ad by a small company. A large advertisement for a small firm may actually outpull a small ad placed by a multibillion-dollar firm. Try such an ad for one year. If it brings in clients, continue to use it. If not, drop the ad entirely or simply maintain a listing.

Former Employers

Many consultants get their initial cash flow going by selling their services to former employers. The rationale is simple: no matter what the circumstances of your departure (unless you were fired for incompetence), you have something to offer that company in expertise and experience. Retaining you as a consultant allows your former employer to use that expertise without the large overhead of an annual salary and benefits, even though the consultant may get a much higher hourly rate than the former employee. A former employer may also wish to hire you simply to ensure that you will not go to work for a competitor, either as a consultant or as a full-time employee. In any case, it is certainly worth exploring. Approach your former employer, explain that you are now going into full-time consulting, and that you would be happy to do for the company what you did in the past, as well as other appropriate work.

INDIRECT METHODS OF MARKETING

Indirect selling methods should definitely be part of your overall marketing program. Their disadvantage, however, is that they are long-term, and usually do not immediately result in billings. Thus, as attractive as they are for building a consulting practice, they cannot be relied on by themselves, especially in the early stages of your business.

Indirect methods of getting clients include:

1. Speaking before groups
2. Sending out newsletters
3. Participating in professional associations
4. Joining social organizations
5. Writing articles
6. Writing a book
7. Writing letters to the editor
8. Teaching a course
9. Giving seminars
10. Distributing publicity releases
11. Exchanging information with noncompeting consultants

Let's look at each of these in more detail.

Speaking Before Groups

This is an excellent way of building your consulting practice. In your community there are numerous groups that use guest speakers, sometimes on a monthly or even a weekly basis. If the type of consulting you do, or something associated with it, is of interest to any group of individuals, chances are you have a product you can present to that group. Pedro Chan, an emigrant from Macao, China, used this method to build his acupuncture consultancy for physicians. You can do the same thing. All you do is pick a topic having to do with the services you offer, whether it's tax consulting, starting a new business, direct response marketing, or some other subject of potential interest. Go to your telephone book and find local organizations that appear to have meetings and therefore may use guest speakers. In each case, ask to speak to the program chairman. Tell that person what you have to offer and how the membership can benefit from your presentation. Make sure your speech is short, explicit, to the point, and relevant for your audience. At the end of your speech, let your listeners know how to contact you for additional information. A business card is good, but a prepared handout, with information on your presentation and your telephone number and address, is even better. In the front of this book you will see "Cohen's Maxims." This is a handout that I give all attendees at my courses and seminars. In the bio you supply to the organization (which they will use to promote your appearance and to introduce you when you speak), make certain you include the fact that you are a consultant. In some cases you will actually get paid for your presentation, but this is only a bonus. The real objective is to gain exposure and eventually get additional clients.

Newsletters

The way to use a newsletter to get clients is not simply to dispense news but to dispense news of interest to potential clients and to remind older clients that you are still around. Every time a client or potential client receives one of these newsletters with your name on it, he or she thinks of you. One method is to use newsletters written by someone else. These syndicated newsletters are mailed out with your firm's name imprinted on each copy. One firm that does this is Cambridge Associates, 137 Newbury Street, Boston, Massachusetts 02116. Of course, you can write your own newsletter with specialized information pertaining directly to services you offer. It doesn't have to be elaborate; you can type a master directly onto your business letterhead, and have a quick-printer reproduce it. If the material is of value to your readers, you can believe it's going to increase your credibility and help to build your practice.

Let me tell you a story about effective use of a newsletter. I was the head of a rapidly growing organization and had been hiring new people every few months, mostly through advertisements in *The Wall Street Journal*. Every time one of my ads appeared, headhunters would call offering to find the needed candidate for me; but since I had never dealt with headhunters and knew that they were expensive (fees up to 30% of an executive's annual salary), I turned them all down. However, one day I received a friendly letter from a certain recruiter, along with a free subscription to his newsletter. Over the next two to three months I continued to receive this newsletter, which I found very professional, and when I next needed to recruit I decided to try this person. That newsletter earned that headhunter a $7,500 fee on that one placement, and much future business as well.

Professional Associations

Membership in professional associations can be an excellent way to obtain clients over the long term, for two reasons. For one thing, your participation lends you the credibility of the association even if you yourself are unknown. Also, professional associations are excellent for making contacts, especially if you take an active role. Plan to participate actively in programs, hold office, etc. Over the years many clients have come to me because of my active role in associations.

Social Organizations

Social organizations are more for contacts than credibility. They can include alumni associations, tennis or bowling clubs, or health studios; I have even obtained clients from fellow members of a martial arts club! When a social relationship is established, a client relationship often follows. Individuals see you, get to know you, and begin to trust you. If they happen to have a need in an area you are consulting in, they may well think of you. With very little direct effort, you have made a sale.

Writing Articles

Naturally, if you are going to write an article, it must have to do with the type of consulting you do, and it must be interesting and valuable to the reader. Perhaps most important of all, the bio that you include with the article must note that you are a consultant.

In fact, the first consulting assignment I ever received was the result of an article I had written for a magazine called *Ordnance*. The executive vice president of one of the largest aerospace companies in the country saw my article, and found it particularly interesting since he had headed a project having to do with the very product that I wrote about. He contacted me immediately for a possible consulting engagement. I heard about another consultant who wrote a single article and syndicated it to 90 different in-house publications, offering each an exclusive in its particular industry. That is, if the article was accepted by a magazine Ford published for its employees, he didn't offer it to Chrysler or American Motors. But there are several hundred different classes of industries, and so the number of publications to which he made this "exclusive" offer was fairly large. The result was so many requests for his services that he had to go into business as a consultant broker, brokering the offers that came his way, because he simply could not handle them on his own.

I've used this marketing method to promote not only my consulting services but other activities as well. One example concerns a book that I wrote, *Building a Mail Order Business*, published in its first edition by John Wiley & Sons in 1982. To assist the promotion of this book, I wrote an article entitled "Can Anyone Make a Million Dollars in Mail Order?" and self-syndicated it around the country to magazines and newspapers, offering each an exclusive in its geographic area or industry. (As long as the publications know what kind of rights you are offering, this is entirely legal and ethical.) In this manner, I multiplied my readership for this one article many times over. One day my publisher called and asked if I would be willing to go on the radio on KLBJ in Austin, Texas, and naturally I agreed. This radio appearance, which was actually done from my office in California through a telephone hookup, led to additional radio and television appearances around the country and in Canada. But the interesting thing is, this first appearance resulted from the article I had written. Someone in Austin had read the article, requested a copy of the book, and felt that it might be an interesting subject for a half-hour talk show.

Two books that may be helpful in the area of marketing and publishing articles are *A Complete Guide to Marketing Magazine Articles* by Duane Newcomb (Cincinnati: Writer's Digest Books, 1975) and *How to Get Published in Business/Professional Journals* by Joel T. Shulman (New York: AMACOM, 1980).

Writing a Book

Writing a book is much like writing an article—except that there is more to it. Having your book published demonstrates expertise in a certain area because the reader knows that your writing has passed a rigorous screening by the publisher. Publication gives you a credibility edge over your competitors who do not write. I continue to receive a considerable number of requests for consulting that result from my books. Recently I had a most unusual request. The president of a small company, who had read both *The Executive's Guide to Finding a Superior Job* (published by AMACOM in 1978 and released in its second edition in 1983) and the mail order book mentioned previously, asked if I would locate a senior director of marketing for his company. Although I indicated that I hadn't done headhunting in some years, this potential client said that he had read both my books and felt that the combination of a former headhunter who was an expert in direct response marketing was just what he needed. The result was my first search assignment in years.

For more information on writing books, see *How to Write "How-to" Books and Articles* by Raymond Hull (Cincinnati: Writer's Digest Books, 1981); *The Book Market: How to Write, Publish & Market Your Book* by Aron Mathieu (New York: Andover Press, Inc., 1981); and *The Non-Fiction Book: How to Write and Sell It* by Paul R. Reynolds (New York: William Morrow, 1970).

Letters to the Editor

Letters to the editor can have the same result as other types of writing: building credibility. To be effective as marketing tools, the letter should contain comments resulting from your expertise in a certain field, and you should identify yourself as a consultant in the area on which you are commenting.

Teaching a Course

Teaching a course at a community college or a university can also lead to consulting assignments. Of course, the course must be in your area of expertise. Also, make sure you teach this course at night, since this is the time when business executives are more likely to be continuing their education. My own teaching has led to major consulting assignments with large companies locally as well as internationally. My only cautionary note here is that you must not consult with individuals while they are your students. This would be a conflict of interest. When I am asked about consulting while I am also serving as an instructor, I indicate that I would be happy to talk about the student becoming a client after the course is over.

Giving Seminars

Giving seminars is much the same as teaching a course. Attendees at seminars tend to be responsible individuals with companies interested in the topic. If your seminar has to do with the area of your consulting services, this can easily lead to additional assignments. I know of several consultants who depend solely on this method to promote their practice; the fees they receive for giving the seminar are only a secondary consideration. You don't even need to do the administrative work of setting up your own seminars. Contact any local community college or university. Many offer seminars and are always on the lookout for new talent. They will require an outline of the seminar that you wish to give, its target market, the hours of attendance, the price, as well as a strong description of your background and your expertise for giving the seminar.

Publicity Releases

Every newspaper, trade journal, magazine, or any other publication depends on a constant flow of news. They are interested in what you have to say, as long as what you have to say is of potential interest to their readership. Any time something of importance happens in your field, there is probably a story in it for some publication. Many times you will be surprised that what you consider common knowledge is new and quite interesting to many people, including potential clients. It is easy to write a publicity release. Just tell your story in a terse, straightforward style like that used in a newspaper article. A potential mailing list for your publicity release should include newspapers and other media such as trade journals whose target readership contains potential candidates for your services. Directories that list such media are available in your local library. Your librarian will be happy to help you find what you need.

Exchanging Information with Noncompeting Consultants

Once you have established your area of expertise in consulting, you will find that there is a noncompeting consultant network made up of other consultants who provide different services, much like doctors who deal in only one specialty and refer their patients to other specialists when required. Let's say that you specialize in organizational development, and a potential client or one of your established clients is seeking marketing consulting. You can recommend another consultant who will be able to help your client. In turn, this marketing consultant can recommend your organizational development services to her clients when needed. To set up this kind of network, use the cold-calling or direct mail techniques described earlier in this chapter, only this time target noncompeting consultants. Offer these other consultants an exchange in which you will recommend their services to your clients or potential clients if they will do the same for you. Make certain that they have a good supply of your business cards and brochures, and ask for the same from them.

It is always important when clients contact you to find out how they happened to get your name. In many cases, this will be a referral, and once referrals begin coming in it is a sure sign that you are well on your way to a successful practice. But in order to know which of the direct methods or indirect methods to continue and which to eliminate, you should always ask the question: Can you tell me how you got my name?

MARKETING CONSULTANT SERVICES
IN THE PUBLIC SECTOR

There is a tremendous opportunity for consultant services in the public sector, consulting for federal, state, or local governments. For the same reasons that large businesses use consultants, the government has a real need for external services and will probably continue to spend millions or even billions of dollars to obtain them. Consulting services used by the government include advice on or evaluation of agency administration and management in such areas as organizational structures and reorganization plans; management methods; zero-base budgeting procedures; mail-handling procedures; record and file organizations; personnel procedures; discriminatory labor practices; agency publications; internal policies, directives, orders, manuals, and procedures; management information systems; program management such as program plans; acquisition strategies; regulations; assistance with procurement of solicited or unsolicited technical and cost proposals; legal aspects; economic impacts; program impact; mission and program analysis; and much, much more. There are also various research and development and technology assessments done by external consultants, even though the government officially does not classify these areas as consulting services.

How Do You Get on the Government Bandwagon?

The basic method of locating opportunities to sell to the government is to use the *Commerce Business Daily* (CBD), a newspaper published by the U.S. government five days a week. It's expensive—a yearly subscription by mail will cost you several hundred dollars—and so I don't recommend that individual consultants order a subscription until their business in the government sector is high enough to warrant it. Fortunately the CBD is also available in many public libraries. Many states also publish business opportunities periodically; for example, the state of California provides the *California State Contracts Register*. Contact the contracting office of your state to see if such a publication is available.

With regard to using the *Commerce Business Daily* or state publications, I recommend that you not bid directly on consulting opportunities unless you have had prior contact with the government agency. Simply responding to an advertisement in the CBD or a similar publication will usually produce nothing but wasted time and money to put the proposal together. You need face-to-face contact with your prospective customers to convince them that you are better than the competition, and rarely can you do this with a proposal alone. The way to use these publications effectively is to consider the advertisements a source of future clients, and to make appointments for face-to-face meetings so that a later request for proposal will find you well prepared.

Another method of locating opportunities in the government is to contact the Small Business Administration (SBA) in your area. Almost every government agency has the need for some type of product or consulting services. Whether or not they need *your* services is another story. That you must investigate. Your local SBA office can help. Let them know that you are a business consultant and tell them your area of expertise. Frequently, they will be able to refer you to someone within their agency who can help you find government contracts. The SBA also hires small-business consultants to help counsel their own small-business clients.

The Buying Process

The government buying process usually begins with an IFB (Invitation For Bid) or an RFP (Request For Proposal). With an IFB, usually you just state a price for whatever is wanted; with an RFP, in addition to a price, you must submit a technical proposal documenting your method for accomplishing whatever services are requested. It is important to recognize that submitting an IFB or an RFP does not guarantee you a contract. Usually other firms are competing for the same work. Low price is always of importance; in fact, with the IFB, low price determines who wins the contract, assuming that the firm is otherwise qualified. With the RFP, however, other factors may be of equal or even more importance. That is one reason why preproposal marketing is so important.

The Importance of Preproposal Marketing

Some years ago I did considerable research on the factors that influence the winning of small government research and development contracts, $2 million or less. Two popular theories seemed to indicate that marketing was more important than technical approach or even the price attached to a particular proposal. One of these was consumer acceptance theory.

According to consumer acceptance theory, the consumer may achieve three levels of intensity in his relationship with any product or service: acceptance, preference, and insistence. To achieve consumer acceptance, the lowest level of intensity, the customer might have had some contact with the product or with some promotional effort. This contact leads to a decision on acceptability. Customer preference suggests a more satisfactory experience over a competing product, and implies that the product will be favored over the competition. Insistence, the highest level of intensity, is the stage in which the customer will take the product almost regardless of price or hardship and will brook no substitution. This stage, according to the theory, can be reached by a full knowledge of the product based upon considerable experience.

The other idea that was important to this application of marketing was the merchandising theory. Merchandising here means fitting the product to the potential customer's wants and needs. According to the main aspect of this theory, merchandising must be the central part of any marketing program. The market must be segmented in order to zero in on a specific customer, and the approach must accommodate the fact that this customer has a number of sometimes conflicting wants and needs that must be satisfied. These wants and needs are influenced by the customer's physical or mental state, his background or conditioning, the immediate situation that confronts him, and, most importantly, what he knows about the product either directly through its use or vicariously through communication with others. These wants and needs are of different relative values and may change. The desire for a particular product is influenced by its accessibility, including such factors as price, the customer funds available, and the effort required to secure it. Suppliers are likely to see a product from an entirely different perspective than the customer. Yet the potential exists to present the product in such a fashion that it does satisfy the most important of the customer's wants, needs, and desires, or to alter the product within certain limits in order to accomplish the same purpose. To do this requires presentation to the customer; feedback from the customer; analysis of the customer's wants, needs, and desires; and calculation of the best ways to satisfy them.

Thus both theories, based on practice in the consumer-industrial world, argued for heavy investment in preproposal marketing for small government-research contracts. And, in fact, actual research with several different companies indicated the tremendous importance of the marketing done before the proposal was ever submitted. During this preproposal marketing, not only would the product or service be sold, but also critical information on how much the customer had to spend, the scope of the activities, and the kind of product or service she expected and thought she would receive would be established and made known to the seller. In some cases, win ratios increased from 0% to 100% by the simple influence of preproposal marketing. My point is, preproposal marketing activities are absolutely critical for selling consulting services to any government agency.

The Marketing Sequence

The sequence of marketing to the government involves six steps, all built around the notion of preproposal marketing.

1. Locate potential clients
2. Screen
3. Visit and make presentations
4. Maintain contact and gather intelligence
5. Prepare the proposal
6. Negotiate the contract

Locating Potential Clients

Potential clients can be located, as mentioned earlier, through the *Commerce Business Daily*, the state register of opportunities, the Small Business Administration, or other government directories. Each and every potential client in the government should be located and a list made.

Screening

The initial screening should be accomplished by telephone. Go right down your list and call each potential client one after the other. Indicate what types of consulting services you provide and try to pinpoint the interests of the potential client. If there is no interest, it is better to establish this now, when the only cost is a telephone call. Finally, try to establish an appointment for a face-to-face presentation. If this must be done at some other location, such as out of state, these visits should be coordinated so that you can make several on one trip.

Visiting and Making the Initial Presentation

For the initial presentation, you should organize yourself ahead of time and know exactly how much time you have. If it's 30 minutes or 45 minutes or an hour or two hours, you should know this ahead of time and limit your presentation to these requirements. Also, ask your contact how many people will be present. This will help you to plan your presentation and to know how many handouts or brochures to bring. I will cover presentations in more detail in a later chapter; for now you should understand that you must organize ahead of time and take enough brochures and other handouts so that all your potential clients can have a copy.

Maintaining Contact and Gathering Intelligence

This is probably the most important part of preproposal marketing; not only do you continue to sell at every meeting, you also learn about forthcoming contracts before they are published in the *Commerce Business Daily* and similar publications. You should also try to learn the scope of activity and how much money is available for these forthcoming contracts. Tell your potential client the approach you would recommend, and why. In some cases these approaches will be incorporated into the RFP. This may seem like giving away ideas to competitors, but actually it's not necessarily bad since you should be better prepared than they to do whatever it was you proposed. At the same time you should be honest and forthright in selling your ideas and disagreeing (tactfully) with your potential client when information stated is at odds with facts as you know them or if the cost will be more or less than the agency anticipates. In this way, by the time that you respond to the proposal, both you and your potential client should understand exactly what is going to be requested, what you are going to propose, and about what these services should cost.

The Proposal

In the proposal, there should be no surprises. It is a sales document, one that confirms your outstanding ability, not a vehicle for presenting something new that you have not discussed with your potential client, even though you may think of something at the last minute. The reason for this is that no matter how lengthy your sales document (and some proposals are no more than a single-page letter), you do not have sufficient space to explain everything in detail. You will probably not be permitted additional verbal discussions once a proposal has been requested, and so you may not be able to explain a new idea sufficiently. Any question that goes unanswered could work to your disadvantage in a competitive review process. Also, no matter how unique and advantageous your new idea might be, time is needed to sell the idea to your potential client's boss. Remember that any bureaucratic organization, including the U.S. government, tends to avoid and minimize risk. New ideas that have not been previously sold during the preproposal marketing phase are high risk from the perception of your potential client. Restate what you have already sold and bid in accordance with the funds and scope of the effort as you uncovered them during your prior contacts.

Two recommended books are *How to Sell to the Government* by William A. Cohen (John Wiley & Sons, Inc., 1981) and *The $100 Billion Market: How to Do Business with the U.S. Government* by Herman Holtz (AMACOM, 1980).

To summarize, clients will not automatically come to you. You must market your consulting services. But if you do this well, in accordance with the guidelines in this chapter, you will soon build a successful consulting practice.

3

SUCCESSFULLY NEGOTIATING THE INITIAL INTERVIEW

In this chapter you are going to learn how to prepare for and conduct the initial interview with your prospective client. Along with general instructions about how to dress and how to act, I will give you essential questions that you must ask in order to learn all you can about the potential assignment, which will eventually enable you to confirm the engagement. In addition, I will point out nonverbal signals to look for and explain what each means, and give you listening techniques that will help you in understanding your client's feelings and intentions.

LOOK AND ACT LIKE A PROFESSIONAL

The first impression you make with your client should be the very best; you can never overcome the effects of a questionable image in your client's mind. In large part this is made up of your appearance and your behavior; you want to look like, and act like, the professional that you are.

Dress is extremely important because it helps you make a good first impression. There are only two rules: dress as neatly as possible, and try to look as much as possible like your client. For most business consulting, a conservative suit and tie for men and a suit for women are appropriate. However, if after several engagements you observe that in your industry a different type of dress is common, follow the second rule and dress like your client. Two good books on the subject are *Dress for Success* by John T. Molloy (New York: Warner Books, 1980) and *You Are What You Wear* by William Thourlby (New York: New American Library, 1980).

In this first interview, you should be professional but not pompous. You should always strive to be friendly and to understand your potential client and build empathy with him. Think back to the different medical doctors you have met over your lifetime. Some are professional and friendly, and you feel a real trust with them. Other doctors, who may be of equal if not greater competence, somehow build a wall between you and them, and you trust them less. The same is true with the business doctor, the consultant. You must maintain a professional attitude, and at the same time you must be tactful, friendly, and empathetic.

SEVEN ESSENTIAL QUESTIONS

During the first interview, there are seven questions that you absolutely must ask in order to better understand the client's problems and also to help you to decide whether to accept the assignment

1. *What problem needs solving?* Whether the client contacted you or vice versa, it is important to find out exactly why the client is seeing you. Something is bothering the client. Some clients will spurt it out immediately; others will say very little, not wanting to reveal the full story until they know more about you. Nevertheless, it is important that you draw them out and understand exactly why they are seeing you.

2. *Exactly what does the client want you to do?* What are the specific objectives of the assignment? Even though in this first interview your primary purpose is to gain information, and even though you are still feeling out the situation, once the reason for the assignment has been determined and you have talked to your potential client at some length about the task, it is important to have objectives explained explicitly. For example, maybe this is a personnel problem; does she wish to decrease employee turnover? Does he wish to increase sales? Is there a problem in new product development, with too many unsuccessful products? Whatever your client's objectives might be, it is important for you to know exactly what they are.

3. *How will you know if the objectives have been met?* At first glance this might seem obvious. If turnover is bad, the objective will be met when turnover is reduced. If sales are not what they should be, the objective will be met when sales increase. And so forth. However, you can easily see that there is much room for a difference of opinion. Will your client be satisfied if turnover decreases 10%, 5%, 1%, or 25%? Or if sales increase 5%, 10%, 15%? What you're looking for here is an exact figure, so that both you and your client will know when the specified objectives have been met.

4. *Are there any particularly sensitive issues that you should watch out for?* Any organization made up of human beings contains political problems of one sort or another. As an outsider attempting to insert yourself into and analyze a particular problem or set of problems, you may stumble into difficult political situations in the organization. For some types of consulting and for some clients, this will not be very important. In others, however, there will be some very sensitive issues that your client will not want you to disturb. Certain individuals or certain subjects may be off limits for interviews. If you are not sensitive to these political issues, you could end up leaving the company in a much worse situation than when you came, even though ostensibly you solved the client's problem. Take pains to ask about and to understand the politically sensitive issues. Pay

attention to detail so that you don't stumble around like a bull in a china shop but rather demonstrate the finesse of a real pro.

5. *Who will be your main point of contact?* Usually it's the individual who contacted you first, but this is not always the case. The only way to find out is to ask. Be certain that you have the name, title, and telephone number of this key individual.

6. *Will there be a backup contact?* Even if your main contact plans to be available throughout the assignment, you should request a backup contact. Your primary contact may have to leave on an unforeseen trip or be absent from the company just when you need an important decision. So you lose time, and you may be forced into making a poor decision that could easily have been avoided. So always ask for the name of someone else in the company with the necessary authority on your project, and get his or her title and telephone number as well.

7. *What authority does each player have?* This is a key question. A player is anyone who has an impact on your engagement. If you do not take the time and trouble to identify the players, their responsibilities, and their authorities, you could find yourself misdirected, either innocently by well-meaning individuals, or deliberately by people in the company who do not wish you—or the individual who hired you—well. Some individuals may give you instructions or even verbal modifications of your contract even though they have no authority. Then you may find yourself in a difficult situation, unable to bill for work requested by someone who had no authority to do so. Of course, beyond the loss of time and money, misdirection of this type could cause you to lose an important client.

Take Notes

Naturally, the only way you will remember all you learn during the initial interview is to take notes. For this purpose I recommend a notebook. I carry mine in my briefcase, and as soon as we start our conversation I take it out and begin to take notes. If I don't understand a point, I ask the client to repeat what was said. Some consultant students have asked if a tape recorder wouldn't be a better way to record this information accurately, but I don't recommend it. A tape recorder is an intimidating device. Information that you are given as a consultant is frequently confidential; somehow pencil and notebook seem less threatening to a client's confidentiality. I have found that clients open up more if you use a notebook and a pencil.

I want to emphasize that in the very first interview you must find out everything that you possibly can. Never hesitate to ask for such information as the company's annual report or product brochures if you feel it will be useful to you. In fact, even after you have returned to your office, do not be afraid to call and ask for additional information if it will help you consider different ways to attack the client's problem.

Don't Give Advice Yet

During the first interview, many new consultants are so eager to help the potential client and show that they recognize both the problem and the solution, they immediately begin talking and giving advice. There are reasons you must not do this. First, you don't really know enough about the situation yet to give advice. This is probably true in 95% of the cases. However, even in the 5% when the answer is obvious to you, do not volunteer anything unless you are already being paid for your time. After you have solved the problem, what reason does the client have to hire you?

I have made this mistake myself. But not anymore. Once a client called me about an exploratory interview, and then suggested that I join him and his wife for supper at a nearby restaurant. The net result was that in addition to an hour during which I answered his questions, for the next two hours he and his wife pumped me for information over a delicious steak and drinks. For about a $30 meal, they received several hundred dollars' worth of consulting. On top of that, because I had solved all their problems during our meeting and meal, they did not hire me. Why should they? Their problems were gone.

Interpreting Body Language

Psychologists have confirmed by research what salesmen have learned intuitively: what a buyer says may be less important than the message transmitted by the way he holds his body when he communicates with you. A potential client who is speaking with you with arms folded across his chest, eyes avoiding yours, and brow wrinkled and fists clenched, is probably feeling threatened by the situation and is not communicating openly with you. You are not getting all the information you could, and the client may not be convinced by what you are saying.

When you observe these physical signs, you should back off and try a different approach—anything to break this attitude and get the client to relax. A sign that you have been successful at this is that the client begins making direct eye contact and leans forward to you. If he looks relaxed, with hands not clenched but open or extended, you have gotten through, and he is probably comfortable with the overall situation and is now ready for more open communication. But if he begins to turn his body away from you, avoiding direct eye contact again, you know he either does not want to discuss the issue you brought up or is suspicious of the particular approach you have taken. Again, you are not getting through. To be successful, you must try a different approach.

Also watch to see if the client strokes his chin or neck, chews the end of a pencil, or leans back with his hands grasped behind the head. This indicates that what you say is being evaluated; the client is listening, and you are getting through. Continue to observe, and you will know whether you should continue that approach or attempt a new one.

Finally, you may observe a ready, almost eager attitude on the part of the client, sitting on the edge of the chair, leaning forward, catching your every word. Clearly, you are making a favorable impression, and the client is demonstrating a readiness to act on your suggestions. This means you've gotten through.

Two excellent books that will help you understand body language are *How to Read a Person Like a Book* by Gerard I. Nierenberg and Henry H. Calero (New York: Cornerstone Library, Inc., 1972) and *Body Language* by Julius Fast (New York: Pocket Books, Inc., 1970).

Listening Techniques

There are certain techniques of listening that will encourage various responses. You should use such techniques to your advantage to draw the client out and obtain all the information you possibly can. Many of these listening techniques you already know, but you should review them to ensure you have them at your disposal and can use them consciously in your client meeting.

If you want to keep the other person talking, neither agree nor disagree with what is being said, but use neutral words in a positive way. "I see" or "How interesting" or even "No kidding" will indicate your interest and encourage your client to continue talking.

On the other hand, if you wish to let your potential client know that you understand the information she has been giving you and want her to move to the next point, you would restate what has been said to you. Say something like "As I understand it, . . ." or "In other words, . . ." and then summarize.

If you wish to probe for additional information at the same time, you must lead the individual toward that information tactfully. Ask questions such as "Why do you think this is so?" or "Why do you think this happened?"

Finally, at some point you will want to summarize the conversation and the ideas you've had. This is extremely important, because you will play back these ideas when you develop your proposal. You should do this recap when you control the interview. Take your time and use your notes to make certain you have it right. You can say, "Now, if I understand you correctly, these are the main objectives that you wish to cover, for the following reasons."

WHAT TO DO WHEN THE INTERVIEW IS OVER

For some very short assignments and some special situations, the client may wish to hire you on the spot. When you sense this—you will learn to recognize it with more experience—simply ask for the assignment. Tell your potential client how you bill and ask if she would like you to help her with the problem. As I will explain in the chapter on contracts, even though this constitutes a verbal contract, it is very important that you follow up with a letter confirming exactly what you will do and the compensation you will receive.

However, many engagements, especially the larger ones, will require a formal proposal and additional analysis on your part to determine the appropriate methodology, the time frame, and the price for your services. Therefore, at the end of the initial interview you will not be in a position to offer a proposal, only to indicate when you will submit a proposal. Always ask if you can call should you have additional questions, if a letter of proposal is satisfactory, or if not, what form the proposal should take. You should also ascertain whether you are the only consultant being contacted or whether your proposal must compete with others. Most government proposals are competitive. Deciding whether or not you wish to bid on a competitive contract is up to you. Many consultants refuse to bid on any type of contract and will politely withdraw if there is competition. My own recommendation is to consider all aspects of the situation, including your probability of winning.

Once you have established that a proposal is requested and when it is due, thank your client, make certain you leave your business card, and depart. If there is no specific deadline for your proposal, make sure you submit it as soon as possible. You never know what changes can take place in just a few days that would alter the demand for your services.

COMPANY AUDIT

To show you the scope of questions that might be useful in an initial interview, I have included as Appendix C a comprehensive checklist of questions, "The Consultant's Company Questionnaire and Audit." Do not think that you must ask each and every question at each initial interview. Also, don't feel that because a question is not included, you may not ask it. In every situation you should modify this list for the particular client before the interview. During the interview, if additional questions seem appropriate, make sure that you ask them as well.

4

HOW TO WRITE A PROPOSAL

If an agreement is not reached during the initial interview (and often it is not), the prospective client will expect a written proposal. In this chapter we're going to find out what a proposal must do and why it is necessary. All the essential elements of a proposal will be listed and explained, and a proposal structure will be provided.

WHY A WRITTEN PROPOSAL IS NECESSARY

A written proposal accomplishes five tasks that are important for you in getting on contract and beginning work as a consultant.

1. *The proposal finalizes the agreement.* Sometimes, even after an excellent exploratory interview, you have not yet made the sale. It is not unusual for a potential client to ask for a written proposal even though he is 90% certain about hiring your services. The proposal, then, is a sales document that ties together all the loose ends and closes the deal.

2. *The proposal documents what you are going to do.* The services you are going to perform in this consulting engagement should be clearly understood by both you and your client. A proposal does exactly that; it spells out in black and white exactly what you are going to do, so there is a documented basis for understanding.

3. *The proposal documents the time frame of your performance.* Just as what you are going to do is important, so is how long you will take in doing it and the time sequencing of each event. Sometimes the client will want to know partial information before the full project is complete. When the client wants information by a certain period, she may not hire you if she is not certain she will get it by that period. Documenting this time frame will help assure your potential client that she will get what she wants when she wants it.

4. *The proposal documents what you are going to receive for your services.* Unless you are independently wealthy, you aren't in business as a consultant just for fun, even though you may enjoy it immensely. The proposal specifies the compensation that you are going to receive for the services you propose to provide. Documenting this compensation can save you much trouble in getting paid later on.

5. *The proposal forms the basis for a contract.* As I will demonstrate

shortly, the proposal can be the basis for a contract. In fact, you can actually turn a proposal into a contract by adding a few sentences.

HOW TO WRITE A GOOD PROPOSAL

There are four points to remember in writing a good proposal.

1. *Keep the structure clear and logical.* I will be discussing this structure a little bit later in the chapter.

2. *Use a professional but friendly style.* When you are submitting a proposal, just as in a face-to-face meeting, be professional but be friendly. In fact, if you are writing a letter of proposal, you can be downright folksy; as long as you avoid stepping over professional bounds, it will only enhance your chances of being hired.

3. *Don't spring surprises in your proposal.* I mentioned this previously, and although it sounds very simple, this is one of the hardest things to do. After you return from your initial meeting, you will frequently get new ideas that are different from what you and your client originally visualized. These ideas may be so good that you find it very tempting to include them in the proposal. Resist this temptation, unless you can check with your client first. There may be other reasons you don't know about why the client cannot accept these new ideas. He may need time to sell this idea to other employees, even superiors in his company. If you surprise him in the proposal, he may not have time to do this. Therefore no matter how good the idea, unless you can clear it with your client before submitting it in the proposal, don't do it yet. You can propose it after you get the contract.

4. *Check before you send.* If at all possible, you should double-check the main points of the proposal with your client. If it's a short letter proposal, call the client and read it to her over the phone. For government contracts and some industrial contracts on a competitive bid, this may not be allowed. However, you should always ask; the worst someone can say is no. It is in everyone's best interest that the proposal be on the right track even before you send it. Don't assume that changes can be made after your client receives it.

THE STRUCTURE FOR A LETTER PROPOSAL

Sometimes, especially with large or competitive contracts, the client will specify the structure of the proposal; this is especially true of the government and large industrial firms. In this case, follow whatever structure is specified. However, a letter proposal will be quite sufficient for most of your consulting engagements. Let's see what one looks like.

Opening

Simply state that you are writing to submit your ideas for the project discussed earlier.

Background

Begin by restating the background of the consulting situation. That is, restate your client's assumptions and other general facts in the case. This reassures the client that he has made an astute analysis of the situation. (If the client's assumptions are not correct, then you must convince him of this *before* submitting your proposal. If the customer is determined to use his assumptions, even if you have told him that they are incorrect and why, then you have a choice. You can use the client's assumptions, or refuse the assignment. If you refuse, be as tactful as possible. The client will respect your stand and may contact you in the future.)

Objectives

You should state the objectives of the engagement precisely. Describe exactly what your client will learn or receive as a result of your work. I like to present these objectives in a way that makes them stand out visually— by using bullets, for example:

- Identify at least three secondary retail markets for new product line
- Develop sales projections for six months and for twelve months
- Recommend staffing increases needed to achieve sales projections

Study Methods

In this section you should describe alternative methodologies for accomplishing the objectives. Discuss the advantages of each alternative, and then indicate which method you propose to use, and why. When you describe the methodology, it is important to consider your audience. If your client is technical, you should use technical language; if not, don't confuse things with technical equations or terms. Stating all the alternatives, even those you do not intend to use, is extremely important, especially if you have competition. Competitors may propose alternative methods, and it is important that you show your client why these methods will not work and why the method you have chosen is the best. If you are convincing on this point, your potential client will use your proposal to help swing others to your way of thinking and to adopt your proposed methodology.

Potential Problems

Any project has inherent in it potential problems that could limit or detract from achievement. Don't omit or gloss over these potential problems; document them clearly, but also state how you will handle them if they occur. Clients smart enough to hire a consultant are smart enough to realize that potential problems exist. You cannot fool them into thinking that your approach is problem-free. In fact, they will respect you more for anticipating the problems, as long as you have thought through what corrective actions you will take.

Data Flow Charts and Product Development Schedules

A data flow chart is sometimes called a PERT chart. PERT (Program Evaluation and Review Technique) was developed for the management of complex multimillion-dollar projects for the government. It shows what tasks you will accomplish and in what order for most efficient management. It is more appropriate for very complex programs, but it can always be included in the proposal. If nothing else, it adds a bit of showmanship to your proposal and demonstrates the control you have over the project. A product development schedule will probably be sufficient for most projects; we will discuss how to build one in a later chapter.

The Finished Product

Your client will want to know what he can expect by way of a finished product. Will you be furnishing a report? A staff study? Photographs? And how many copies will you provide? This can be important, because frequently the client will need to distribute the information to others, perhaps the board of directors or other managers in the company. Specify exactly what you will furnish and what it will contain, the number of copies, drawings, photographs, and other details. Include the date that you will complete your study and submit your final report.

Cost and Payment Information

For most small contracts, it is not important to break down cost information unless the client requests it. However, the timing of payment is important. The client will want to know not only how much you want but when you want it. For example, do you want 50% of your fee up front and 50% at completion; or one third at signing of contract, one third at some intermediate point, and one third at completion; or work-in-progress billing with monthly invoices; or are you willing to take everything in one lump sum when you submit your report? (The last, by the way, is not recommended.)

CONVERTING A PROPOSAL INTO A CONTRACT

The last paragraph is a close. It can—and should—be friendly, but it can also serve as a contract if you combine it with an authority to proceed. Here's how to do this in a friendly but professional way.

> Please simply sign at the bottom where indicated, for authority to proceed under these conditions, and return the original to me. However, if you have any questions or suggestions pertaining to this proposal or the work you would like accomplished, please do not hesitate to call me at 555–1234.

If you decide to use the suggested last paragraph and allow it to be converted into a contract, you may wish your attorney to review this information.

An example of a letter proposal is shown in Figure 4–1, and a more extensive proposal is in Appendix D.

Figure 4-1. A typical letter proposal.

April 24, 1985

Mr. Joseph Black
Unique Sales Co., Inc.
4571 Plainview Avenue
Pasadena, CA   91107

Dear Mr. Black:

We enjoyed the pleasure of meeting with you on Wednesday, April 18. We were amazed to learn that you had been in the mail-order business for over 33 years selling government surplus.

The purpose of this letter is to present our proposal for a research study based upon the objectives discussed in our meeting with you.

Please keep in mind that this is a proposal and subject to your ideas and suggestions.

A RESEARCH PROPOSAL FOR:

An Investigation of the Seasonal
Sales Trend of Unique Sales Co., Inc.

Background

Unique Sales Company is a mail-order company that sells to individual consumers as well as to governments of foreign countries. The company originally sold marine equipment but has now expanded its sales to other items, such as aircraft parts, auto parts, and hydraulics.

Unique Sales Company's main objective was to sell government surplus items; however, recently there has been a drastic cut in the availability of government surplus items.

The sales trend of this company has its peak months around the first five to six months of the year; the other months are slow. In the eastern part of the U.S., the sales are very much affected by the weather. The more severe the winters are, the higher the sales are, because people stay at home and read the sales catalog.

Objectives

The primary objective of this study would be to gain an insight into the factors causing cyclical variations in sales for the mail-order industry and for Unique Sales specifically. Recommendations for Unique Sales' actions will be made upon evaluation of data collected.

More specifically, the following areas would be investigated:

I. Sales trends (cross section)
    A.   Industrial-oriented mail-order house
    B.   Consumer goods-oriented mail-order house
    C.   Industrial/consumer-oriented mail-order house
II. Factors affecting sales
    A.   Weather
    B.   Product line
    C.   Target market
    D.   Advertising effectiveness

Study Methods

Several market research methods would be incorporated into this study.

The first would be an exhaustive search for all readily available secondary market statistics and data. This would be statistical information already published or obtainable at a nominal cost. Possible valuable sources for this information would be U.S. government agencies, trade associations, the National Weather Bureau, and trade periodical publishers, as well as the standard business bibliographies.

In addition, personal telephone calls would be made to selected individuals in this industry. These would be those recognized as the most knowledgeable in the industry. From these telephone calls an attempt would be made to obtain data not uncovered during the search for secondary information.

Potential Problems

In most secondary research studies, the existence of relevant market statistics and data cannot be determined until the actual study is begun.

Market statistics do not exist for all industries and, in some cases, exist only in the files of private firms. In these cases, the information is considered proprietary and is not generally released to the business community.

In many instances, the use of personal interviews can compensate for lack of published data and bring to the forefront valuable data otherwise not available.

Overall, even with possible information gaps, the research team is confident we can supply Unique Sales Company with a viable, well-documented report.

The Report

Our report would consist of a description of the study objective, design, and the findings reported at three levels of detail.

First would be what we see as the major findings or highlights of the study, including our conclusion and recommendations. This section would be followed by a more detailed and documented discussion and analysis of the findings. An appendix would contain brochures and other supplementary materials.

Cost and Timing

The cost of this completed study would be $1500, one-half payable on authorization to proceed and one-half payable on delivery of final report, two copies of which will be delivered in its final form.

The study will be compiled, and the reports delivered, four weeks after authorization to proceed.

We know that you are busy. Therefore simply sign below for authorization for us to proceed with this work. If you have any questions or suggestions to make regarding this proposal and the proposed study, please feel free to call us at once.

Sincerely yours,

_____

W. W. Smith
Director of Research

_____

Mark Tizon
Principal Consultant

Authorization to Proceed

I agree to the terms in the above proposal and grant authorization to proceed in accordance with these terms.

_____

Mr. Joseph Black
President
Unique Sales Company

5
PRICING YOUR SERVICES

Pricing is crucial. As well as determining the size of your billings and profits, it has a definite effect on your image. In this chapter we're going to look at the three basic pricing strategies available to you as a new consultant and different methods of billing for your services.

THREE PRICE STRATEGIES

The three basic price strategies available to you are a low-price strategy, a high-price strategy, and a meet-the-competition strategy. Let's look at each one in turn.

A Low-Price Strategy

A low-price strategy is basically penetration pricing. The idea is that you will enter the marketplace with a price lower than your already established competitors; you will attract clients because of your bargain prices. This strategy can work for new consultants, and with it you will be able to attract more business than you could otherwise.

However, there are some serious shortcomings. First, since with consulting you are basically selling your time, you will have to work harder than those established in your profession to make the same amount of money. This also means that your competitors will have additional financial resources to use in counter-marketing campaigns if they choose. Secondly, price has an image connotation. In the minds of many, low price means cheap, and a low-priced consultant may be viewed as a low-quality consultant. You may be given only the less rewarding, grubbier types of assignments and not those that require high exposure with top-level management. Finally, after choosing a low price, it may be extremely difficult to raise your price later on as your practice grows.

For example, I have a friend, George W., who is a CPA specializing in tax consulting. When George first started out as an independent consultant, it was part-time and after-hours. To build his practice, he chose a low-price strategy; his billing rate was only $15 an hour. Some years later, after his part-time practice had grown, George quit his full-time job and bought an established tax consulting practice, the clients of which were billed at $35 an hour. George now had two prices, $35 an hour for new clients and $15 for old. Since he was now full-time, it seemed to make sense to raise his fees to his demonstrated worth of $35 an hour. However, as soon as he did this, every one of his former $15-an-hour clients quit or threatened to. George needed these clients, so he reversed himself and maintained two different prices. However, he was hardly comfortable with this solution. First, he felt he was cheating his new clients by charging them 71% higher. But George also felt he was cheating himself, since he clearly was now worth the higher figure even if his older clients wouldn't pay it. George brought this problem to me for advice. My suggestion was to raise the lower prices slowly, and to give a more acceptable reason than the fact that "he was worth more." So George raised his price 10% or 15% every year, blaming rising costs and a high inflation rate. In a couple of years the amount charged his lower-priced class of customers was close enough to the higher-priced class that he could finally accept the loss of those clients that refused to go along with the final increase.

A High-Price Strategy

Another option that any consultant has, whether new or old, is to adopt a high-price strategy. This one is somewhat more risky. You are telling the world that you are worth that money; your image is one of a high-quality consultant. However, your potential clients may or may not believe you. It goes without saying that you had better be what you advertise. The high-price strategy is, however, a viable one that many new consultants overlook, either because they are afraid they are not worth the money, because they somehow have a nagging feeling they are ripping off their potential client, or because they fear they will get no business if they choose to charge high prices. The truth is that in many cases you are not only worth much more than you think, but may be worth more than established consultants who are already earning big fees. Before you reject a high-price strategy, consider the following stories; they are all true.

· My student Harry S. graduated with his MBA from California State University at Los Angeles and went to work for a major consulting firm. The day after he left the university, the firm that hired him billed Harry's time at $1,000 a day plus $300 overhead, a total of $1,300 a day.

· Several years ago I got together with two friends. One had been the city manager of a major U.S. city and had retired into consulting; the other was general manager of a division of a major aerospace company. The former city manager said, "Boy, this consulting is great. Do you know that I'm getting $50 an hour?" I should add that this friend had more than 30 years' experience as manager of various cities and also had a PhD. At the time I was billing $100 an hour, and I said, "Bob, you are not charging nearly enough. I'm billing at twice what you're billing at. I'm billing at $100 an hour." The general manager of the aerospace company looked at both of us and smiled. "You're both undercharging," he said. "We pay our consultants $250 an hour, and to my knowledge none of them is as qualified or as good as either one of you two."

· Several years ago I received a telephone call from an individual who identified himself as Jerry S., a former student at my university. Jerry said that he had been referred to me, even though he had not been my student, and that he had graduated eight years previously with a bachelor's degree. He explained that he and his partner gave seminars for companies on management styles and had put together a workbook for the seminars. Since I was known as an expert in direct response marketing, he wanted some advice on how they might self-publish this workbook and sell it through the mail. During our talk, I became intrigued with Jerry's frequent mention that his clients were top management, and I finally asked him who his clients were. "Oh," he said, "we give special seminars for small groups of top management in each company. Usually there are no more than five to seven in each group." I asked about his pricing. "Oh, we go high, for image purposes," Jerry replied. "We charge $7,000 a day." I laughed and told him that he understood the marketing of his services very well. Seven thousand dollars a day was far above the average prices charged by many providing similar services who held PhD degrees.

· A friend of mine, Mary T., was going to start a part-time consulting business doing copyediting for writers. I told her of my concern that people generally charge too little for their services, and I gave her a short talk on not being afraid to use a high-price strategy. At the time of this incident, copyediting services were going for approximately $10 to $15 per hour. A week later she told me she had her first client—at $40 an hour. I almost fell over when I found out how much she was receiving, and so did she when I told her that her client was paying four times the amount usually charged by experienced copyeditors.

Note that in all cases these consultants had little difficulty getting the higher fees they charged. In fact, the clients were quite ready to pay them. Again, the reason is the image value of the consulting services offered. Therefore, if you are good at what you intend to do as a consultant, do not be afraid to use this pricing strategy. Far more consultants err by choosing the low-price than the high-price strategy. It is not a ripoff if you are good at what you do. In fact, in many cases, you will find that clients will not even want to engage your services if you charge too low a price, since they will feel that either your work is weak or you are inexperienced.

Therefore, even from the standpoint of idealism and wanting to do the greatest amount of good, consider the high-price strategy.

A Meet-the-Competition Price Strategy

This means simply that you choose a price that is approximately the same as your competitors or potential competitors are charging. If you choose this particular strategy, you must offer something else in addition to your regular services. Otherwise, why should anyone deal with you? But if you do offer some differential advantage, and if you promote it to your potential clients, the meet-the-competition price can be a viable strategy. Differential advantages may include quicker service, specialized additional service not offered by anyone else, around-the-clock availability to answer consulting needs, quicker results, or better results.

If you are going to choose this strategy, spend some time thinking through your differential advantage; what additional service can you offer above and beyond your competition?

OTHER CONSIDERATIONS

Two other considerations should be taken into account when you are considering your pricing strategy: industry pricing, and client price adjustment.

Industry Pricing

Certain industries have accepted prices for certain services. It is very difficult to violate this norm and build a viable practice. For example, some employment agencies will find workers, professional or otherwise, for their client companies. On receipt of a job order, they will send the client several candidates to interview. If one of their candidates is hired, the agency may be paid 10%–15% of the individual's annual salary. Executive search firms will supply three or more candidates for a particular job; if one of their candidates is hired, they will get up to 30% of the executive's annual salary. Sometimes they will get paid whether one of their candidates gets hired or not. They perform essentially the same service, but note the significant difference in pricing. Therefore, when you are developing your fee schedule, it is important to consider the industry you are in. Employment agencies are simply not going to be paid the same as search firms, no matter how good a job they do. Of course, you can deviate from the normal industry pricing, but it's difficult, and in any case you must first consider the norm for your industry.

Client Price Adjustment

Some consultants charge different amounts to different clients, depending on who they are or how big they are. For example, sometimes the government (federal, state, or local) has certain restrictions on the amount it can pay consultants, by policy or by law. If you expect to do a lot of government work, this will affect your pricing strategy.

Similarly, small companies generally cannot afford to pay as much as large companies. The examples I gave you earlier—the aerospace company that paid consultants $250 per hour and the consulting firm that billed the recent graduate's time at $1,000 a day—were large companies. Clearly, smaller companies cannot pay these kinds of fees. You are therefore faced with a decision about billing if you deal with both large and small firms. You must either have billing based on the size of the company, have one low price for all, or have one higher price for all. The higher price eliminates a certain segment of your potential market. So may the lower price, because of image. A two-price system may also lead to problems. You must make this decision yourself, considering all the factors in your situation.

METHODS OF BILLING

Basically there are four different methods of billing:

1. Daily or hourly
2. Retainer
3. Performance
4. Fixed-price

Let's look at each.

Computing Billings Daily or Hourly

Billing on a time basis is fairly common with consultants, but deciding whether to bill on an hourly or a daily rate takes some consideration; as with so many other things, it's a tradeoff. Some consultants feel that just getting started on any project will take the better part of a day, so they won't bill at less than a full day's rate. Even if a client wanted just two hours of their time, they would bill their daily rate as a minimum. Other consultants, especially those who work part-time and others who want maximum flexibility in their scheduling, use the hourly rate. Billing hourly lets them work at home or at some other location, work for a couple of hours on one project and a couple of hours on another, and in that way work with several clients in a single day. Of course one can also bill for fractional hours.

If you are considering a daily or hourly rate, be very certain you don't price yourself so low you can't make a decent living. Even if you elect to go with a penetration-price strategy, be very careful when you set your fee. Sometimes new consultants get into the field simply because they do not want to work for someone else. They are perfectly willing to work for the same amount that they made at their previous job. At first glance, that seems perfectly logical. However, using your previous salary to set your hourly rate is a trap you should avoid. Let's try out some numbers (pay attention; this is important).

Let's say you are currently making $32,000 a year and your fringe benefits are worth another $3,000; that's a total of $35,000 a year. If you work 40 hours a week times 50 weeks (considering that you will have two weeks' vacation), that's 2,000 hours a year; $35,000 divided by 2,000 is $17.50 per hour. So should your billing rate be $17.50 an hour? Absolutely not! It is very important to understand that this figure does not take into consideration the fact that when you are working on your own, you will have overhead to contend with. Even though you'll try to keep this overhead as low as possible, I think you'll be surprised how fast it adds up. For example, let's make the following assumptions about your yearly expenses.

Clerical support	$3,600
Office rent	6,000
Telephone	2,400
Automobile	6,000
Insurance, benefits, etc.	5,600
Marketing expenses	18,400
Entertainment	1,600
Professional dues and subscriptions	800
Accounting and legal fees	2,400
Miscellaneous	2,400
TOTAL	$49,200

Therefore, to receive $35,000 income a year, the same that you got working for someone else, you must charge $35,000 *plus* the $49,200 overhead, for a total of $84,200 a year. That works out to $42.10 per hour. If you want to tack on a profit for your firm (if it is incorporated), over and above your salary, you must add something to this figure. If you want a profit of 10%, you now have a billing rate of $46.31 per hour. That's what you must charge yourself to earn the same salary you were making when you worked for someone else.

Working on Retainer

With a retainer you receive a constant monthly fee, in return for which you guarantee a certain number of hours will be available to your client. This has advantages for both sides. For you, it gives a guaranteed income and cash flow, which can be very advantageous. In fact, most consultants would be willing to take a retainer at a reduced fee in order to ensure that money was coming in every month. For your client, a retainer guarantees that you won't work for a competitor and that the client will get first priority on your time. An additional advantage to you is that if the hours are not used, you get paid anyhow.

Performance Billing

We'll discuss performance contracts in a later chapter. Basically this means no money without results. For example, for every dollar saved through your recommendations you might get 25%. Keep in mind that:

1. Performance billing is a good marketing tool.
2. It's critical to put all terms in writing.
3. It's a mistake to tie performance to profits, since profits can be manipulated for accounting or taxation purposes.

Fixed-Price Billing

A fixed-price contract, which we talked about earlier, is one in which you agree to do a certain job and get paid a fixed amount for it. The number of hours you work on the project is entirely up to you; you must put in whatever it takes. With a fixed-price contract you can make more money, but at a greater risk, since you must guarantee accomplishment.

In order to be profitable on a fixed-price contract, you must be sure these five points are followed:

1. Give yourself a "pad" in your estimations; overestimate a little to allow for miscalculations.
2. Use good estimating techniques, as discussed in the chapter on scheduling.
3. Control your costs closely.
4. Document carefully exactly what you are required to do.
5. Get all changes to the contract in writing.

There are some basic formulas for setting the fee in a fixed-price contract; a typical one is shown in Figure 5–1. In this formula, overhead has

Figure 5-1. Basic formula for a fixed-price contract.

Four elements of the formula are:

1. Direct Labor
2. Overhead
3. Direct Expense
4. Profit

Sample Computations

Direct Labor

Consultant	12 days @ $150/day	=	$1800
Assistant	4 days @ $90/day	=	360
Secretary	5 days @ $56/day	=	280
			2440.00

Overhead   (65% of direct labor)   1586.00

Direct Expense

Air Travel	300	
Rental Car	100	
Special Printing	90	
Per Diem/Travel	110	600.00

                                            Subtotal   4626.00

Profit (12% of subtotal)   555.12

                                            Total Price $5181.12

been included as 65% of direct labor. Obviously you must cover your overhead some way; this percentage method is an attempt to spread your annual overhead among your various clients. You do this by estimating what you think your yearly overhead expenses will be, converting that into a percentage of your estimated annual income, and then adding that percentage amount onto the labor costs of each contract. In this case, a billing rate of $50 an hour would yield $100,000 annual income; estimated expenses of $65,000 a year works out to 65% for overhead. This particular formula incorporates a profit of 12%. The profit percentage is somewhat arbitrary, although it may be regulated in government contracts or contracts with firms that limit consultants' profit by policy.

DISCLOSING THE FEE

Sometimes only one of the different ways of presenting the fee to the client is acceptable. Some clients will not accept a daily or hourly rate; they prefer a fixed-price contract. Therefore, it is a good idea to calculate your fee using *all* the various methods. If one way is unacceptable to your client, try another. However, in disclosing the fee, it is generally best to provide the minimum amount of financial data required. Therefore, for a fixed-price contract, if possible I indicate only the bottom-line price; in the example in Figure 5–1, I would say the price is $5,181.12. Or, if I am billing on a daily rate, I would give just that rate—$1,200 a day plus expenses, for example.

Some clients, especially the government, will require full disclosure. In this case you will have to make a full presentation, such as that in Figure 5–1, showing exactly how your figures are arrived at. The average client probably doesn't care about your overhead. Certainly there is no value to you in divulging your overhead so that potential competitors could discover it as well. Simply include it within your daily or hourly rate or within the fixed price if your fee is stated in this fashion.

6

WHAT YOU MUST KNOW ABOUT CONSULTING CONTRACTS

This chapter explains why consulting contracts are necessary and shows you how to develop your own. It also explains the different methods of incurring a contractual obligation, the different types of contracts, and the major elements of any contract. Finally, a sample contract is provided to help you develop your own contract.

WHY A CONTRACT IS NECESSARY

Essentially, a contract covers two very important bases for you.

1. *It ensures that you and your client both understand fully the services you are to perform.* For your part this will prevent wasted time, wasted resources, and wasted effort. It will also help ensure that you have a happy client at the end of the engagement. And a happy client will give you more work in the future, and good referrals to others.

2. *It will help you get paid.* Always keep in mind that even though you really enjoy your work, you must get paid in order to survive. Consulting may be a lot of fun, but without getting paid you won't be around to enjoy it. Having a written contract that documents your compensation will help you to gently remind your client of the financial obligations. If all goes sour and you must sue to get paid (this rarely happens, but it could), a signed contract is almost a necessity.

DEVELOPING YOUR OWN CONTRACT

It is most definitely possible to develop your own standard consulting contract and to use it in every situation with only minor changes regarding the particular client, services, and compensation. We will talk more about this later, but note now that you should have your attorney assist you with this. Do not, however, dump the whole project on your attorney; it will cost you excessively. A better procedure is to develop each element your-self, using the information in this chapter, and rough out the contract the way you would like it. Use the sample contract in this chapter as a guide.

Once your rough contract has been formulated, have your attorney review it and put it in final form.

If Your Client Has a Standard Contract

Sometimes your client will be a large corporation with a standard contract. You may be asked to use this contract rather than yours. Naturally, the final decision is always up to you. You should have your attorney review it, but usually these contracts are not unfair and you may find them entirely acceptable.

METHODS OF INCURRING A CONTRACTUAL OBLIGATION

There are five basic ways that a consultant can enter into a contractual obligation:

1. The formal contract
2. The letter contract
3. Order agreements
4. Purchase orders
5. Verbal contracts

Let's look at each of these in turn.

The Formal Contract

The formal contract is a written document describing the obligations of both parties. For most assignments I would recommend that you formalize your engagement in this way. It will save you many problems, heartaches, lost fees, and misunderstandings later on. Figure 6–1 shows a sample contract, the basics of which I used in contracting with a major multibillion-dollar corporation.

The Letter Contract

A letter contract can be evolved from a proposal. It is in written form, but it is much simpler than a formal contract. However, it contains the basic elements of the contract, and though it may look like a letter, it qualifies as a contract.

Figure 6-1. Form for a sample consulting contract.

CONSULTANT AGREEMENT

AGREEMENT made _____, between _____,
                        date   name of client
with principal offices at _____
                                    client's address
hereinafter called "Client" and _____
                                          name of consultant
of _____hereinafter called "Consultant."
      consultant's address

　　　1. <u>Services.</u> Consultant, as an independent contractor,
agrees to perform, during the term of this agreement, the
following services: _____

_____

_____

_____

under the terms and conditions hereinafter set forth.
　　　2. <u>Products.</u> The term "Products" shall mean the client's line
of _____.
　　　3. <u>Compensation.</u>
　　　(a)　Client shall pay Consultant at the rate of __ per hour
for each hour that Consultant shall perform services during the
term of this Agreement; provided that the number of hours does
not exceed _____
without the written consent of Client.
　　　(b)　In addition to the hourly compensation provided
herein, Client agrees to pay Consultant _____under the
following conditions: _____

_____

　　　4. <u>Term.</u> The initial term of this Agreement shall commence
on the _____ day of _____, _____ and end on the last
day of _____, _____, provided however that either
party may terminate this agreement at any time during the initial
term or any extension term by giving the other party _____
days notice in writing.
　　　This Agreement may be extended beyond the initial term or
any extension term only by the written agreement of both parties
prior to the expiration of the initial term or any extension.

5. <u>Designation of Duties.</u> Consultant shall receive his requests for services to be performed from

_____ , _____ , _____ .
client's name   title   company and address

6. <u>Restrictive Covenant.</u> During the term of this Agreement, Consultant shall not make his services available to any competitor of Client in the specific field in which he is performing services for Client.

7. <u>Indemnity and Insurance.</u> Consultant shall indemnify and hold harmless Client, its officers and employees against all losses, claims, liabilities, damages and expenses of any nature, directly or indirectly arising out of or as a result of any act or omission by Consultant, its employees, agents or subcontractors in the performance of this Agreement.

If Consultant uses, or intends to use, a personal automobile in the performance of this Agreement, Consultant shall maintain throughout the term of this Agreement automobile liability insurance in accordance with the law of the State of _____ and not less than _____

_____ .

8. <u>Patent Rights.</u> Consultant agrees during the term of this Agreement and for a period of 12 months after the termination of this Agreement, to assign to Client, its successors, assignees, or nominees, all right, title and interest in and to all inventions, improvements, copyrightable material, techniques and designs made or conceived by him solely or jointly with others, relating to Products, in the performance of this Agreement, together with all United States and foreign patents and copyrights which may have been obtained thereon, and at Client's request and expense, will execute and deliver all proper assignments thereof.

9. <u>Confidentiality.</u> Consultant shall not disclose, publish or authorize others to publish design data, drawings, specifications, reports or other information pertaining to the work assigned to him by Client, without the prior written approval of Client. Upon the expiration or sooner termination of this Agreement, Consultant agrees to return to Client all drawings, specifications, data and other material obtained by Consultant from Client, or developed by Consultant, in connection with the performance of this Agreement.

10. <u>Reimbursable Expenses.</u> The following expenses will be billed in addition to compensation:

Figure 6-1 (cont.)

      (a) Travel expenses necessary in order to perform services required by the Agreement. Use of personal automobile will be billed at __¢ per mile.

      (b) Telephone, telegraph, and telex charges.

      (c) Computer charges.

      (d) Printing and reproduction.

      (e) Other expenses resulting directly from performance of services in the Agreement.

      11. Warranty. Consultant services will be performed in accordance with generally and currently accepted consulting principles and practices. This warranty is in lieu of all other warranties either expressed or implied.

      12. Limitation of Consultant Liability. Client agrees to limit any and all liability or claim for damages, cost of defense, or expenses against Consultant to a sum not to exceed $_____, or the total amount of compensation, whichever is less, on account of any error, omission, or negligence.

      13. Payment Terms. Terms of payment are as follows: _____ due on the signing of Agreement and _____ due _____. _____ due on delivery of _____. A _____% per month charge will be added to all delinquent accounts. In the event Consultant shall be successful in any suit for non-payment, Consultant shall be entitled to recover reasonable legal costs and expenses for bringing and maintaining this suit as a part of damages.

IN WITNESS WHEREOF, the parties have signed this agreement.

                                _____

                                      Consultant

                                _____

                                        Client

Order Agreements

Order agreements have the force of contracts. They are typically used for the purchase of consulting services to be accomplished over a period of time. They commit both you and your client to contractual terms before work is authorized. For example, an order agreement may commit you to so many hours of consulting over, say, a year's period; it also specifies how much you will be paid. However, your client decides when to initiate the agreement. In other words, an order agreement ties both you and your client to terms but not necessarily to a start date. In some cases the order agreement will be combined with an option, which gives the client flexibility on whether or not to actually use these services. But if the services are used, the terms are as set forth in the order agreement.

Purchase Orders

A purchase order is an internal form authorizing you to do work and to bill for it. It is generally used by larger firms to acquire relatively low-cost products or services. Consulting services may be "ordered" on a purchase order rather than a formal contract because your client can do this quickly and simply, as compared to going through the formal contractual process, which could involve your client's legal staff and some time delay. Usually purchase orders have a limit specified by company management, say, $25,000 or under.

Verbal Contracts

Always remember that a verbal contract is still a contract. Verbal contracts are very common in consulting, but they are not always desirable and definitely not recommended in two situations: with new clients, and for large projects. If the nature of the consulting situation with a new client is such that a more formal written contract is not possible, try to get a significant part of the payment up front before you start work. Also, be very clear with your client; spell out your objectives, what you are going to do, and how and when you are going to do it.

TYPES OF CONTRACTS

There are four basic types of contracts in consulting, each with variations:

1. Fixed-price contracts
2. Cost contracts

3.   Performance contracts
4.   Incentive contracts

There is no one best contract for all situations, but rather a one best contract for a particular situation. Therefore, it is important to know the advantages and disadvantages of every one of these contracts.

The Fixed-Price Contract

A fixed-price contract is one in which you agree to do a certain job for a predetermined amount. With few exceptions, no price adjustment is made after the award of the contract, regardless of your actual cost in performing it. You the consultant assume all the cost risk. If your estimate is poor, you could actually lose money on a fixed-price contract. On the other hand, if you can reduce the cost below the original estimate, you have the potential for making increased profit. Therefore, the more certain you are of your cost and your potential for reducing it, the more willing you should be to take a fixed-price contract. Conversely, the more difficult it is to estimate a particular job, the more risk you assume and the less willing you should be to accept such a contract. With all types of contracts, it is important to have an accurate estimate, but with the fixed-price contract it is crucial.

Cost Contracts

In a cost contract, you are paid on your actual cost of performing the services; that is, your time plus related expenses such as the cost of reproducing your reports. As long as you put the time in, you are paid.

Obviously this type of contract involves a very low risk to you as a consultant. However, some clients will not accept cost contracts; they want to ensure that the project is actually completed within a certain budget. Thus, even when costs are difficult to estimate, you may have to choose between a fixed-price contract and no contract at all. One solution may be to break the overall task into subtasks. Those subtasks that you can cost out with minimum risk, you can take under a fixed-price contract; others, under a cost or a performance type contract (performance contracts will be described shortly). Another solution may be to insert a "not-to-exceed" clause in the contract, so that you are paid for the work you actually do, but the client is guaranteed that your fee will not be higher than an agreed-upon amount.

The cost contract has several variations, two of which—cost plus fixed fee, and cost plus incentive—are frequently used by the government for research and development projects. With the fixed fee type of cost contract, the consultant is paid a total of the cost plus a fixed amount agreed to by both parties prior to performance. With the incentive fee type, the consultant is paid the cost plus a variable incentive fee tied to different levels of performance agreed to in the contract. The incentive type of performance contract is discussed in more detail in the next section.

Performance Contracts

Pure performance contracts are rare. More commonly, they may be made a part of a modified cost or fixed-price contract, wherein increased performance may earn a higher fee or reduced performance a lower one. However, by themselves, performance contracts are useful in closing a deal (more about that later).

With a performance contract, your payment is based solely on actual performance. An executive recruiter who works on contingency—that is, he receives a fee only if one of the candidates he recruited is hired by his client—is actually working on a performance contract. Performance contracts can also be based on an increase in sales, a decrease in turnover, or other measurable factors. One cautionary note here: Do not accept a performance contract based on profits. Profits have too many definitions and are too easy to adjust upward or downward for accounting and taxation purposes. Although you may have done a great deal to increase performance, it may not show up in accounting profits at the end of a year.

I mentioned earlier that pure performance contracts are rarely used except to close a deal. Here's how to use a proposed performance contract to help you come to terms with your potential client. Let's say you have been negotiating with a prospective client, and while he seems satisfied about most aspects of the project, he is not quite ready to finalize and sign a contract with you. Perhaps you have been thinking along the lines of a fixed-price contract, which you have costed out at $5,000. To close the deal you could say something like this: "Look, Mr. Smith, I am absolutely convinced that I can do this job for you and do it within the time period and at the price I indicated. However, I can see that you are hesitating, so let me make an offer that I don't think you can refuse. Let me design this marketing campaign for you and if it doesn't increase your sales by at least 25%, you pay me nothing. However, if your sales increase by 25% or more, and I have every confidence that it will be more, then you will pay me the $5,000."

You can see how the performance contract works. Either you perform or you receive nothing. That's why it's such a great close during negotiations. Your prospective client thinks, "Well, now, if this individual is ready to take a performance contract, what have I got to lose? He must be convinced." Strangely—and this is the kicker—your client will usually agree to *your original terms* rather than the performance terms.

Incentive Contracts

Incentive contracts are also tied to performance. A type of incentive may also be combined with a fixed-price or cost contract, based on achieving certain pre-set objectives or goals. When setting these goals, you must help your client; be certain that the incentive fee structure is not unrealistic on either side. Remember that you are trying to build a long-term relationship, and terms that are unreasonable to you or your client, even if agreed to at the time, could lose you business in the future.

A client of mine once asked me to help him increase attendance at his seminars. In return, I would receive, in addition to a fee, an additional $20 for every seminar attendee above an agreed minimum (which was his maximum the previous year). I was to receive this $20 bonus not for just this one seminar, or even all similar seminars in a single year, but for life. That is, as long as these seminars were given by my client and the attendance was higher than the previous year's top, with no increase in costs, I was to receive $20 for each and every attendee above that number, whether or not I performed any additional services for this company. In my opinion, these terms were unreasonable and unfair to the client. We finally restructured the compensation, retaining an incentive contract in which I would be reimbursed with a fixed amount up front and then an amount for each seminar attendee over the minimum; however, I would get this for three years, not for the rest of my life.

ELEMENTS OF A CONTRACT

There are five basic elements that should go in any contract:

1. *Who*. Who is the consultant, who is the client, and who are any other parties that are in any way involved in the project?
2. *What*. What services are to be provided to the client?
3. *Where*. Where are these services to be provided? What is the address of the client, what is the address of the consultant, and are there special locations involved in the consulting?
4. *When*. When are the services to be performed, and when is compensation to be paid?

5. *How much.* How much does the consultant receive for his services?

In addition to these five basic elements, other important conditions of the engagement should also be covered. These include:

- Competitive restrictions
- Patent right
- Insurance coverages
- Confidentiality

A SAMPLE CONTRACT

Look again at the sample contract in Figure 6–1. Note how the contractual elements fit in. You can use this sample as a basis for developing your own contract. Don't forget to have your attorney go through it, to ensure that everything applying to your situation has been taken care of and that your rights are fully protected.

7
PLANNING AND SCHEDULING THE CONSULTING PROJECT

Planning and scheduling of all but the simplest of consulting engagements are absolutely essential. Not only are these steps necessary for preparing the proposal, but once on contract, having a firm and good schedule in hand will save you time and money and will increase the quality of your performance as a consultant. All organizations I ever worked with that had problems with project management have had one outstanding thing in common—a failure to properly plan and schedule their projects before they began to work. Proper scheduling is not difficult. In this short chapter I am going to give you a special form that will help you do this.

Refer to the project development schedule in Figure 7–1. Start with the column headed "Task." Your first job is to list every task associated with the consulting project that you intend to undertake. Next, figure out how long each task will take to complete, in days, weeks, or months (in Figure 7–1, the numbers at the top of the columns represent whichever time period you choose), as well as hours. Note that the measurements of task *length* and task *time* are not identical. A market research survey may require 80 hours of labor, which would be two weeks of eight-hour days. An organizational audit that required interviews with 20 different company executives might take four calendar weeks to complete (because of the difficulty of scheduling executive time) but only 40 hours of your time.

You will also need to decide who will accomplish each task. If you are doing all the work yourself, this is easy. But in some cases you will have other consultants or even other organizations working for you.

Figure 7–2 shows a project development schedule in which the tasks have been determined. After you write each task down on the schedule, draw a double horizontal line, starting when the task will begin and continuing to the right until the task is complete. Consider each horizontal row as being either days, weeks, or months after the authority to proceed. (Note that in the example in Figure 7–2, the time period being used is months.) Later, when you get the contract, you can write the actual days, weeks, or months in and use this schedule to manage the project. Convert the hours into dollar expense for each period, and total both hours and costs. Use a diamond figure like this ◊ to indicate critical dates, a time when something of great importance to the project must occur, such as the date a report is due. (Later, when the critical task is complete, you will

Figure 7-1. Form for a project development schedule.

TASK	1	2	3	4	5	6	7	8	9	10	11	12
TOTALS												

Figure 7-2. Proposed project development schedule, showing tasks and hour and cost estimates.

MONTHS AFTER AWARD OF CONTRACT

TASK	$50/Hr 1 Hrs/$	2 Hrs/$	3 Hrs/$	4 Hrs/$	5 Hrs/$	6 Hrs/$	7 Hrs/$	8 Hrs/$	9 Hrs/$	10 Hrs/$	11 Hrs/$	12 Hrs/$
Development of Research Tool	20/1000											
Secondary Data Collection	10/500											
Interviewing		20/1000	20/1000	20/1000	20/1000	20/1000	20/1000					
Data Recording		2/100	5/250	5/250	5/250	5/250	5/250	3/150				
Data Analysis and Computations			5/250	5/250	5/250	5/250	5/250	10/500				
Follow–Up Interviews			2/100	3/150	2/100	1/50	1/50	5/250				
Final Report Preparation									40/2000			
TOTALS 269/$13,450	30/1500	22/1100	32/1600	33/1650	32/1600	31/1550	31/1550	18/900	40/2000			

Report due end of ninth month after award of contract

Figure 7-3. Project development schedule, after project initiation.

TASK	Hours F/A* June	Hours F/A* July	Hours F/A* Aug.	Hours F/A* Sept.	Hours F/A* Oct.	Hours F/A* Nov.	Hours F/A* Dec.	Hours F/A* Jan.	Hours F/A* Feb.	Hours F/A* Mar.	Hours F/A* Apr.	Hours F/A* May
Development of Research Tool	20/18											
Secondary Data Collection	10/13											
Interviewing		20/16	20/21	20/16	20/	20/	20/					
Data Recording		2/3	5/6	5/5	5/	5/	5/	3/				
Data Analysis and Computations			5/4	5/4	5/	5/	5/	10/				
Follow-Up Interviews			2/3	3/3	2/	1/	1/	5/				
Final Report Preparation												
TOTALS	30/33	22/19	32/34	33/28	32/	31/	31/	18/	40/			

New estimated completion date

Report due March 1

*Forecast/Actual

color the diamond in like this: ♦.) In Figure 7–2, a project development schedule has been filled in up to this point.

Once you are on contract and have the authority to proceed, you can use the schedule as indicated in Figure 7–3. On a new form, substitute the actual dates for the estimated time periods. (On Figure 7–3, note that month 1 is replaced by June, month 2 by July, etc.) Copy on to your new form the double horizontal lines that show when each task will begin and end. As you proceed to carry out the contract, shade in portions of the rectangular block formed by the double line to show the percentage of the task completed. At the end of each month fill in actual hours worked on each task and compare with hours forecast. If you know that a task must be delayed for some reason, adjust your schedule by the use of a triangle and a series of dashed lines as shown.

Using the project development schedule will demonstrate to your potential client that you know what you are doing and that you have carefully thought through the entire consulting project. It will give you a much better chance of having your letter proposal accepted. Once on contract, using the schedule as a management tool will assist you in controlling and avoiding slippages and cost overruns. You will have more happy customers and fewer ulcers. If others besides you are involved in any part of the contract, it will also alert you well ahead of time if any of the support people are overdue.

8
HOW TO SOLVE YOUR CLIENT'S PROBLEMS EASILY

In this chapter I am going to show you a logical, step-by-step approach to problem-solving. This methodology does more than help solve problems; it will also organize your thinking process, and provide an outline for presenting your analysis, conclusions, and recommendations to your client, both as a written report and as a formal, in-person presentation. I am going to cover every step in detail, and then show you a sample problem that you can work yourself, including forms to assist you. Then we'll go over the solution to this problem and analyze the results.

THE HARVARD CASE STUDY METHOD

The technique I'm going to show you is commonly known as the Harvard Case Study Method of Problem-Solving; it is also known in the military as the Staff Study Method. It is a structured, step-by-step process of considering and analyzing the various alternatives available to solve a problem, and honing in on the one best solution. Let's take a look at the six elements of this method.

1. Central problem
2. Relevant factors
3. Alternative courses of action or solutions, with advantages and disadvantages of each
4. Discussion and analysis of alternatives
5. Conclusions
6. Recommendations

Defining the Central Problem

Defining the single central problem in a particular situation is the single most difficult, most important task in consulting problem-solving. If you correctly identify the main problem in a situation, you can find many different approaches to solving it. But if the wrong problem is identified, even a brilliant solution will not correct the situation. You are well advised to take all the time necessary; be sure you are indeed looking at the central problem.

One of the major errors that new consultants make in defining the central problem is to confuse the symptoms with the problem. For example, low profits are not a central problem, but a symptom of something else that is the central problem. Frequently a consultant will be on a case with many different problems; in fact, there usually is more than one problem. The object then is to locate the *main* problem in the situation, the one that is more important than any other and is therefore "central." If you find more than one major problem in a particular situation, you should handle each one separately.

Once you have identified the central problem, you should write an initial draft of what the problem is. Try to keep this statement as simple as possible by making it as short as you can—a one-sentence central problem is usually best. Be aware, however, that even if you have spent some time in both identifying the problem and wording it as concisely as possible, in many cases you will have to go back and modify it as you proceed through the analysis.

Also be careful not to word the problem as if it were the solution, by assuming one particular course of action is correct before you analyze it. Remember, too, that your goal is to develop as many different courses of action as possible. Try not to word your statement so that only two alternatives are possible. For example, don't ask the question "Should a new product be introduced?" That allows for only two alternatives: yes or no. Occasionally there are some situations where only two alternatives need be analyzed. Usually, however, you can reword the problem statement so that you open it up to more than two courses of action.

In your statement, include important specifics about the problem. "What should be done about the possibility of introducing a new product?" is not the best problem statement. It allows for more than two alternatives, but omits specifics about the problem that may be important to readers of your report who are not as familiar with the problem as you or the individual who hired you.

Be careful about making your problem statement too long, by incorporating various additional factors. Even if these factors are relevant, they will make the problem statement unwieldy, awkward, and difficult for any reader to understand.

With these cautionary notes in mind, begin formulating your problem statement. Phrase it as a question, beginning with "who," "what," "when," "where," "how," or "why." Or you may start with an infinitive, as in "To determine the best source for borrowing $10,000."

List Relevant Factors

Note that this section of the structure speaks of "relevant factors." Both words are important. Relevant because, even though there will be many different factors in any situation, you are to determine and list only those that are relevant to the central problem you have decided upon.

In this task you will be listing "factors"—not just facts. You may include estimates, computations, assumptions, and even educated guesses, in addition to facts. Naturally, if one of your relevant factors is not a fact, you should label it accurately as an assumption, an estimate, or whatever, so that you won't mislead anyone.

List Alternatives

In this section you will list every alternative, solution, or course of action that could possibly solve the central problem. Then list the advantages and the disadvantages of each one. It is at this point that frequently you must go back and modify your central problem statement. You may think of a solution that is excellent, but not a solution to the central problem as you originally wrote it. If you want to include this course of action, you must restate your central problem so that it fits with this alternative. This is important: each alternative solution or course of action listed must potentially solve the central problem as you have stated it.

Although theoretically it is possible to have an alternative with all advantages and no disadvantages, this is highly unlikely. If this were the case, the solution would be self-evident and this problem-solving procedure would be superfluous.

Analyze the Alternatives

In this fourth section, you will analyze and discuss the alternatives thoroughly in light of the relevant factors you have listed. As you proceed, additional relevant factors may come to light. If so, go back and add them to your list. However, the focus of this section should always be to compare, and discuss in detail, the relative importances of the advantages and disadvantages of each course of action. For example, one course of action may have disadvantages that are unimportant when measured against the relevant factors. Or, an alternative could have advantages that are very important.

At the end of this discussion and analysis section, and even as you are doing the analysis, certain conclusions will start to become obvious. Don't state these conclusions in the discussion and analysis section, however; save them for the next section. In fact, here is an accurate test of the clarity of your thinking so far: show the entire analysis up to this point to someone who is not particularly familiar with the problem. Have him or her read your central problem, the relevant factors that you have identified, the alternative courses of action with the advantages and disadvantages, and finally your discussion and analysis. Then ask him what his conclusions are. If they are identical to yours, you have correctly worded your discussion and analysis. If his conclusions are different, you have made an error either in the wording of the discussion and analysis, or in the logic of your conclusions.

List Your Conclusions

In this section list the conclusions that you arrive at as a result of your discussion and analysis. Do not add any explanations; they belong in the previous section. Also, don't list conclusions based on information extraneous to your analysis. Your conclusions are based solely on your discussion and analysis. Another common error here is to restate relevant factors as conclusions.

Make Recommendations

In this section you explicitly state the results of your analysis and your recommendation on what your client should do to solve the central problem you have defined. As with your conclusions, do not include extraneous information or explanations; always remember that explanations go in the discussion and analysis section. If you are presenting this orally, your client can always ask additional questions; if this is a written report, your client can always contact you for additional information. However, if you have done the analysis correctly, there will be no need to explain your recommendations; your reasons will be obvious from your discussion and analysis.

Many consultants first learning this methodology ask about the difference between conclusions and recommendations. With a recommendation, you put your reputation on the line. You make it clear and unequivocal what you want your client to do. You are accepting full responsibility for the recommendations you make. A conclusion is written in the passive tense—"Marketing research should be done." Recommendations are written in the imperative—"Initiate marketing research." If a conclusion on your list read, "A new accountant should be hired," the recommendation would be, "Hire a new accountant."

THE CHARLES BENSON PROBLEM: A CASE STUDY

Now we're going to try a problem, using the methodology just discussed. Assume that the client is the chief engineer of the Zeus Engineering Company and has come to you for consulting advice. You are to analyze the chief engineer's problem, define it explicitly, and, using the methodology we just went over, make recommendations to him. The problem situation is fully described in Figure 8–1. Figure 8–2 contains forms that will help you use the structure to arrive at the solution. The solution and a step-by-step critique are contained in Figure 8–3. Do not read the critique until you work the problem in detail. Time spent now will pay dividends later on in learning to use and apply this problem-solving methodology.

Figure 8-1. A description of the Charles Benson problem.

Charles Benson, 35, had been employed as a design engineer for the Zeus Engineering Company for seven years. He was a reliable employee as well as a skillful and inventive engineer. Seeking to earn additional money, he decided to pursue his own business evenings and weekends. His products were similar to those made and sold by Zeus Engineering. Benson's supervisor found out about Benson's business, but took no action for several months, believing that the business probably would not amount to much and that eventually Benson would drop it. However, one afternoon Benson's supervisor found him using company time and a company telephone to order materials for his business. The supervisor reprimanded Benson on the spot and warned him that such practices would not be tolerated. He also said that the incident would be reported to the chief engineer. A few days later Benson received written notice from the Chief Engineer that he must divest himself of the business within the month or resign from the company.

A month later, Benson's supervisor asked him directly for his decision. Benson stated that he had thought it over and talked with friends as well as officers of his union, and decided that he would not give up the business, nor would he resign. He argued that he was a good employee, and that his outside company did not interfere with his work for Zeus Engineering. The small amount of business that he did could not hurt the company, and he was neither using company resources, nor soliciting its accounts. Therefore, what he did with his own time was of no concern to the company. Benson's supervisor reported the conversation to the chief engineer.

You are the chief engineer. What action should you take?

Adapted from "Theodore Thorburn Turner," a case in *Principles of Management*, 4th ed., by George R. Terry (Homewood, Ill.: Richard D. Irwin, 1964), p. 222.

Figure 8-2. Form to use in solving the Charles Benson problem.

CENTRAL PROBLEM _____

_____

_____

_____

_____

RELEVANT FACTORS (List) _____

  1. _____

  2. _____

  3. _____

  4. _____

  5. _____

  6. _____

  7. _____

  8. _____

  9. _____

10. _____

11. _____

12. _____

13. _____

14. _____

15. _____

ALTERNATIVE COURSES OF ACTION

1. _____

_____

Advantages:

  A. _____

  B. _____

  C. _____

Disadvantages:

  A. _____

  B. _____

  C. _____

2. _____

_____

Advantages:

  A. _____

  B. _____

  C. _____

Disadvantages:

    A. _____

    B. _____

    C. _____

3. _____

_____

Advantages:

    A. _____

    B. _____

    C. _____

Disadvantages:

    A. _____

    B. _____

    C. _____

4. _____

_____

Advantages:

    A. _____

    B. _____

    C. _____

Disadvantages:

    A. _____

    B. _____

    C. _____

5. _____

_____

Advantages:

    A. _____

    B. _____

    C. _____

Disadvantages:

    A. _____

    B. _____

    C. _____

DISCUSSION/ANALYSIS _____

_____

_____

_____

_____

Figure 8-2 (cont.)

_____
_____
_____
_____
_____
_____
_____
_____
_____
_____
_____
_____
_____
_____
_____
_____

CONCLUSIONS (List):

1. _____
2. _____
3. _____
4. _____
5. _____
6. _____
7. _____
8. _____
9. _____
10. _____

RECOMMENDATIONS OR DECISIONS (List):

1. _____
2. _____
3. _____
4. _____
5. _____
6. _____
7. _____
8. _____
9. _____
10. _____

Figure 8-3. A solution to the Charles Benson problem.

CENTRAL PROBLEM

Begin by zeroing in on the central problem; this may require several attempts.

1. *Should Charles Benson be retained as an employee of the Zeus Engineering Company, or fired?* This way of stating the problem limits the solutions to two courses of action— retaining or firing.
2. *What should be done about Charles Benson?* This statement lacks specifics about the problem that are important if the analysis is to be presented to someone else.
3. *What policy should Zeus Engineering set regarding employees establishing outside businesses?* This may be a problem that needs to be worked on, but its solution disregards specifics of Benson's case, including the earlier warning.
4. *What to do about Charles Benson's outside business considering the fact that he was warned, that the union may take action, that he has been a good employee and a superior engineer?* This one tries to incorporate all the relevant factors, resulting in an unwieldy and awkward statement of the central problem.
5. *How to keep Charles Benson with Zeus Engineering?* This statement assumes one alternative course of action as the solution before the analysis is done.
6. *What action should be taken regarding Charles Benson's outside business activities?* This is a simple, concise statement of the central problem.

RELEVANT FACTORS

Facts

1. Charles Benson has been a superior engineer and a reliable employee prior to the problem.
2. Benson has been with the company seven years.
3. The products that Benson makes are similar to the products made by Zeus Engineering.
4. Benson's supervisor knew about the business but took no action for several months.

Figure 8-3 (cont.)

5. Benson was caught by his supervisor doing business on company time, and using a company telephone.
6. Benson was ordered by the chief engineer, in writing, to drop the business or resign from the company.
7. Benson states that he will not give up the business or resign from the company.

Assumptions

1. Benson has stated that he has contacted union officers and that they support his position. This is presumed to be true.
2. Benson states that he is not soliciting company accounts. This is presumed to be true.
3. Benson's current level of business will probably not hurt the company in the sense of his being a competitor. Nor will his present product line directly compete with Zeus Engineering's product line.
4. It is assumed that Benson's business activities are no longer done on company time, and that his outside work does not currently interfere with his work at Zeus.
5. Current company policies do not specifically forbid an outside business, although conflict of interest laws, secrecy clauses, and the company's ownership of ideas resulting from company work have an impact on the legal aspects of the problem.
6. Benson is not a key employee, in the sense that his leaving the company will of itself have a major negative impact on the company.

ALTERNATIVE COURSES OF ACTION

1. Discharge Benson.

Advantages
1. Will enforce discipline since Benson was warned that he must give up the business or resign.
2. Will discourage employees in the future from starting outside businesses.
3. Will solve any problem of conflict of interest arising from the nature of Benson's business.

Disadvantages

1. May lead to union problems, considering their current support of his position.
2. May lead to a morale problem if it is believed by other employees that the company has acted unfairly.
3. Will lose a superior engineer and an otherwise reliable employee.

2. Retain Benson.

Advantages

1. Will avoid any problem with the union.
2. Will retain a superior engineer and an otherwise reliable employee.
3. Will avoid any feeling among other employees that Benson is being treated unfairly.

Disadvantages

1. May result in a discipline problem, since Benson was ordered to give up the business or resign.
2. May eventually result in a direct conflict of interest due to the nature of the products and the customers.
3. Will effectively establish a company policy on this matter that may not be desired.
4. Will encourage other employees to start outside businesses.

3. Discharge Benson as an employee, but retain him as a consultant. (The mechanism for the discharge should be Benson's resignation.)

Advantages

1. May avoid any problem with the union.
2. Will reward Benson for past performance as a superior engineer and otherwise reliable employee.
3. Will maintain discipline, since Benson was warned that he must give up the business or resign.
4. Will solve any problem of conflict of interest arising from the nature of Benson's business.
5. Will avoid setting policy or precedent regarding employee businesses.

Disadvantages

1. May encourage other employees to become consultants rather than employees with the company.

Figure 8-3 (cont.)

2. May set policy of a different kind: that employees who start their own businesses will be retained as consultants.
3. May not solve the problem if Benson refuses to resign to accept a consultancy.

DISCUSSION/ANALYSIS

1. Several important issues bear on this problem:
   A. The disciplinary issue, and the fact that Benson was told to resign or to divest himself of his business.
   B. The importance of fair treatment and its potential effect on other employees. Benson has been a "superior engineer and otherwise reliable employee." There is currently no conflict of interest and no further misuse of company time is anticipated.
   C. The policy issue. If Benson is retained, this will tend to set policy and may encourage other employees to similarly start businesses on their own.
   D. Potential union involvement and a legal suit.
2. All of these issues are important and must be considered in the decision. Therefore:
   A. Discharging Benson should be avoided since it has considerable potential for affecting the morale of other employees (who may consider it unfair treatment of a superior and otherwise reliable employee who made one "mistake") and because it could lead to problems with the union and a legal suit.
   B. Retaining Benson should also be avoided because of its potential effect on discipline and its tendency to set policy and encourage other employees to start their own businesses.
   C. Discharging Benson as an employee, but retaining him as a consultant, is the only solution that is not negatively affected by the main issues.
3. If Benson fails to accept the solution of resigning to become a consultant, then he should be discharged. Under these circumstances there is less chance of his treatment being perceived as unfair. While the company still risks union problems and a lawsuit, discipline will be maintained, no

policy on outside businesses will be set, and other employees will not be encouraged to follow in Benson's footsteps.

CONCLUSIONS

1. Discharging Benson as an employee, but retaining him as a consultant, is the best solution considering the major issues involved.
2. If Benson fails to resign to accept a consultancy, he should be discharged.
3. The consultancy solution must be presented to Benson as the only all-around fair solution, and not as punishment, in order to maximize his accepting it; however, it must be presented in such a fashion that other employees recognize that resigning or discharged employees are not automatically hired as consultants.
4. A policy on outside employee businesses should be established and publicized as soon as possible.

RECOMMENDATIONS

1. Discharge Benson as an employee and hire him as a consultant.
2. If Benson fails to accept this solution, discharge him immediately.
3. Establish and publicize a policy on outside employee businesses as soon as possible.

9

THE IMPORTANCE OF ETHICS
IN CONSULTING

Ethics is not just a vague theory but a working concept that can have an important and real effect on your consulting practice. This chapter explains why the application of ethics to a consulting practice is so important. You will see that ethics is not simply a matter of obeying the law; it goes much beyond this. You will also see that the ethical problem is not simple, and yet it is one you will face frequently during your work as a consultant.

BUSINESS ETHICS ARE NOT ALWAYS CLEAR-CUT

If ethical questions could be expressed in clear terms of black or white, decisions on corporate conduct would be easy. But that is seldom the case. Let me tell you about a few situations, some of which are well known, where decisions of business ethics were not at all straightforward.

Ethics versus Jobs: The Lockheed Case

The Lockheed payoff scandal—Lockheed executives were found to be bribing Japanese officials to secure contracts for their aircraft in Japan—is even today pointed to as one of the most infamous examples of corporate law-breaking and lack of corporate ethics. Without commenting on the legal aspects of this case, one could inquire into the motivation of those Lockheed executives who made the decision for these payoffs. After all, it was not simply a case of payoffs for personal profits. If the contracts had been lost, thousands of jobs would have been lost—not by the executives concerned but by the workers and managers at lower levels. Therefore, while I do not suggest that this was necessarily the motivation for the payoffs, I do think that if ethics is defined as a set of moral principles for the greater good, then the bad of the payoff must be balanced against the good of job retention for thousands of Lockheed workers.

The Ethics of Marketing Research

Marketing research can be completely honest and aboveboard. However, marketing research is frequently competitive research, and that presents an opportunity for questionable practices. Let me tell you about my own introduction into this field.

As a newly promoted manager of research and development, I studied the possible solution of one of the problems my company faced. Because the business was heavily government-oriented, our production was a continual series of peaks and valleys. The government orders all came during one part of the year, and then we would become extremely busy, producing like mad to fulfill our contracts. Other parts of the year, we had practically no business at all, and our workers were idle. The choices in such circumstances are usually pretty limited. We could try to manufacture our products for someone else, or retain our workers and pay them for essentially doing nothing, or fire our work force every year. None of these solutions was very attractive.

Obviously if we could find some other product to make, which would fill the valleys when no government work was under contract, this would solve the problem. Our company was very much involved in fiberglass protective products such as pilot helmets. One additional fiberglass product that we considered was personal protective body armor for military and police, but we knew very little about this market. To learn more, we decided to hire a marketing research firm—that is, an independent consultant. Bids were requested from several of the leading firms in our area. The firm that won the opportunity to undertake this task had a fine proposal and a good reputation.

One aspect of the research bothered me. Since the information we required involved the total size of the market along with competing products, sales, and other proprietary information, I wondered how such information could be obtained. As I recall, I even commented to one of the executives of the research firm that I didn't know how they were going to get this information, since obviously they couldn't just call up a company and ask for it.

Two months after the contract had been initiated I was given a final report of several hundred pages, along with a personal presentation by a representative from the marketing research firm. The information they provided was exact, precise, and explicit. They had all the information about our potential competitors, the size of the market, the sales, and even in some cases strategies that the competition intended to follow in the coming years. I was amazed at the detail. Innocently, I asked where such information could be obtained. I was told that it had been done in a very straightforward fashion. The researcher had simply called the president of every firm in the business and identified himself as a student doing a report on the unusual product of body armor. In almost every case this researcher

had gotten complete information that was highly secretive and proprietary.

How do you rate that research technique? How would most people?
Let's find out. Washington Researchers is a well-known consulting firm
that does competitive research on companies, products, and strategies. It
also conducts seminars around the country on how to accomplish various
types of competitive research. Several years ago I had the good fortune to
attend one. As a part of the seminar, all attendees participated in a survey
of company information techniques. This survey was developed originally
because participants had asked Washington Researchers for judgments
about the ethics of various means of company information-gathering.
Washington Researchers decided that the issues were too complex to allow
for easy answers. So they decided to conduct this survey as a simple measurement of individual and company practices.

Please stop at this point and take this questionnaire (Figure 9–1),
which asks your opinion about several research techniques or strategies.

Figure 9-1. Washington Researchers survey of company information techniques.

During past seminars, participants have asked Washington
Researchers for judgments regarding the ethics of company
information-gathering. There are too many complex issues
involved to allow easy answers, but we have decided to attempt
a simple measurement of individual and company practices. For
the purposes of this questionnaire, *assume that you are asked
to find out everything you can about the finances, products,
marketing strategies, etc. of your company's closest
competitor.* Several research techniques or strategies are listed
below. Please respond to each by indicating the following:

1. Would your company encourage or condone the use of
   the technique?
2. Aside from your company's policies, would you
   (personally) feel comfortable using the technique?
3. Do you believe that other companies in your industry
   would use the technique in trying to find information
   about your company?

Note: If unemployed, answer question 1 in each series about
a company you would like to work for.

Research Strategy Alternatives

A. Researcher poses as graduate student working on thesis. Researcher tells source that dorm phones are very busy, so researcher will call back rather than having phone calls returned. In this way, researcher's real identity is protected.

   1. Would your company use this technique?   Yes _____ No _____

   2. Would you personally use this technique?   Yes _____ No _____

   3. Do other companies use this technique?   Yes _____ No _____

B. Researcher calls the V.P. while s/he is at lunch, hoping to find the secretary who may have some information but is likely to be less suspicious about researcher's motives.

   1. Would your company use this technique?   Yes _____ No _____

   2. Would you personally use this technique?   Yes _____ No _____

   3. Do other companies use this technique?   Yes _____ No _____

C. Researcher calls competitor's suppliers and distributors, pretending to do a study of the entire industry. Researcher poses as a representative of a private research firm and works at home during the project so that the company's identity is protected.

   1. Would your company use this technique?   Yes _____ No _____

   2. Would you personally use this technique?   Yes _____ No _____

   3. Do other companies use this technique?   Yes _____ No _____

D. The competitor's representative is coming to a local college to recruit employees. Researcher poses as a student job-seeker in order to learn recruiting practices and some other general information about the competitor.

   1. Would your company use this technique?   Yes _____ No _____

Figure 9-1 (cont.)

    2. Would you personally use this
       technique?   Yes _____   No _____

    3. Do other companies use this
       technique?   Yes _____   No _____

E.   The researcher is asked to verify rumors that the competitor is planning to open a new plant in a small southern town. The researcher poses as an agent from a manufacturer looking for a site similar to the one that the competitor supposedly would need. Researcher uses this cover to become friendly with local representatives of the Chamber of Commerce, newspapers, realtors, etc.

    1. Would your company use this
       technique?   Yes _____   No _____

    2. Would you personally use this
       technique?   Yes _____   No _____

    3. Do other companies use this
       technique?   Yes _____   No _____

F.   Researcher corners a competitor employee at a national conference, such as the one sponsored by the American Marketing Association, and offers to buy drinks at the hotel bar. Several drinks later, the researcher asks the hard questions.

    1. Would your company use this
       technique?   Yes _____   No _____

    2. Would you personally use this
       technique?   Yes _____   No _____

    3. Do other companies use this
       technique?   Yes _____   No _____

G.   Researcher finds an individual who works for the competitor to serve as informant to researcher's company.

    1. Would your company use this
       technique?   Yes _____   No _____

    2. Would you personally use this
       technique?   Yes _____   No _____

    3. Do other companies use this
       technique?   Yes _____   No _____

Used with permission of Washington Researchers, Ltd., Washington, D.C. 20007, (202) 333-3499.

Results from more than 500 professional marketing, planning, and business researchers at seminars around the country are contained in Figure 9–2.

An Executive Recruiting Story

Along the same lines, I would like to tell you this story about executive recruiting. The neophyte executive recruiter (headhunter) has two tasks. One is to cold-call companies, as described earlier, in order to obtain what are known as job orders—the authority to do a search. The other task is to identify candidates with the qualities specified by companies and to recruit for the position. Both components of this task are challenging.

This particular neophyte headhunter was told to cold-call a list of potential clients and get as many job orders as he could and then to start recruiting candidates for these jobs. Naturally not all the companies called were in need of a headhunter's services, and some of the contacts were not particularly polite. One of the companies this neophyte called was the "Dynamic Petroleum Company," whose vice president of engineering gave a most memorable response. He began to yell and shout and curse at the headhunter, saying that he never dealt with headhunters, that no one in his company was permitted to talk to headhunters, that he fired any of his engineers or even his secretary for talking to headhunters, and that furthermore, if he was ever called again he would institute legal action. With that, he hung up. This so unnerved the neophyte that he was observed by the president of the search firm, who said, "Let me show you how to handle this. A guy like this isn't a client; this is the source of our product. These are the people that we recruit from."

Five minutes later, the president phoned that same vice president at Dynamic Petroleum. He said that he was a college student whose professor had told him to contact one of the petroleum engineers at Dynamic, that he had forgotten this engineer's name, and that he was afraid to call his professor back. Over the next half hour, this vice president of engineering proceeded to read off the names of over 150 different petroleum engineers in his organization, describing them by specialty, background, and years of experience. He gave away an immense amount of intelligence, which was ultimately used against him, for now his engineers could be contacted by name for recruiting purposes.

I once told this story to a group of approximately 50 middle to senior managers. Several commented on the lack of ethics of the search firm president. But one individual present was himself president of a search firm. He protested, "But that's the business. That's how it's done. You can't do the business if you don't operate in this way."

Again, I don't want you to draw any conclusions about my personal

Figure 9-2. Washington Researchers survey: typical results.

Percentage of "Yes" Responses

Question A			Question E		
	1.	39%		1.	36%
	2.	46%		2.	36%
	3.	86%		3.	80%
Question B			Question F		
	2.	63%		1.	63%
	2.	65%		2.	60%
	3.	86%		3.	91%
Question C			Question G		
	1.	41%		1.	35%
	2.	47%		2.	36%
	3.	88%		3.	80%
Question D					
	1.	33%			
	2.	38%			
	3.	71%			

Used with permission of Washington Researchers, Ltd., Washington, D.C. 20007, (202) 333-3499.

feelings about these matters one way or the other, but merely consider that at least some people in this profession consider this practice at least common, if not ethical.

A Japanese View of Duty

Peter Drucker tells the story of a large Japanese firm that wanted to open an American plant. After an investigation of many locations in several different states, a suitable site was located. So important was this operation that a special ceremony was scheduled, with the governor and many senior state officials and the CEO from Japan.

The Japanese CEO spoke fairly good English; however, to ensure that everything he said would be absolutely correct, an American of Japanese descent was hired to translate his speech into English. With dignity and measured tones, the Japanese CEO began to speak, noting the great honor to his firm to be able to locate in the United States with mutual benefits to his firm and to the surrounding citizens. He also discussed the benefits to the local economy and to Japanese-American friendship. And then, nodding in the direction of the governor and other state officials, he added, still in Japanese, "And furthermore, Mr. Governor and senior officials, please understand that we know our duty and when the time comes that you retire from your honored positions, my corporation will not forget and will repay you for the efforts which you have expended in our behalf in giving us this opportunity."

The Japanese-American translator was horrified. Instantly, she made a decision to omit these remarks in her English translation. The Japanese CEO, who understood enough English to realize what she had done but not why, continued his speech as if nothing had happened. Later, when the two were alone, the executive asked his translator, "How could you exclude my reassurances to the governor and officials? Why did you leave this important part out of my speech?" Only then could it be explained that what is ethical, even a duty, in Japan is considered unethical and corrupt here.

General Electric, Westinghouse, and Allis-Chambers

Some years ago when jet turbine engines were first being developed, General Electric, Westinghouse, and Allis-Chambers formed what would technically be considered a cartel. Cartels, of course, are illegal under the antitrust laws of this country, and this one was eliminated. This is another instance where the law and ethics might be considered at odds, because when the cartel broke up, prices went up, with a resulting drop in demand, bringing a considerable loss of jobs and the eventual bankruptcy of Allis-Chambers. Again, a question here. I don't recommend either breaking the law or establishing cartels, but which was the more ethical conduct?

TYPICAL PROBLEMS OF ETHICS IN CONSULTING

In the practice of consulting, you will eventually be involved in numerous ethical questions. Fortunately, some of them can be anticipated. Consider the following questions from my own seminars and courses on consulting. Usually there is no simple answer, although some are easier to resolve than others.

1. *Client already knows the answer he wants to his problem.* This typically occurs when a client requires an outsider to confirm information that she already knows. For example, you may run into a situation such as the one I described in Chapter 1. Suppose a division of a company has already done a very thorough internal study that suggests the division should get into the such-and-such business. However, because this study was done by the division itself, it is suspect. Top management may wish to have an independent study by a consultant. You may be engaged by that division of the company, and yet the client will make it very clear to you what answer she expects. Do you accept such a consulting engagement or not?

Some consultants say it doesn't make any difference. You're getting paid to do the study even if the answer is known. If the client makes it very clear at the beginning that what she expects is a yes answer, that's what she's paying for and that she'll get. Other consultants take the position that they will do the job and provide whatever answer results from their analysis. If the client insists upon having a yes answer and nothing else (usually this insistence is not stated explicitly, but is very subtle), they will refuse to undertake the study.

There are many different issues to consider, including your need for cash and possible additional business from this client later. But there is no right answer. You have to consider it yourself, and my only advice is to think about the alternatives now, because you will almost certainly encounter it.

2. *Client wants you to omit information from your written report.* This generally occurs when you have included information in your report that your client feels will hurt him with others, either inside or outside his company. After reviewing your report in draft form, he may ask you to delete certain information. Some consultants take the position that they will decide how to handle this based on relevance to the central issue. If the information is not relevant, they will exclude it. Otherwise, they will refuse. However, other consultants feel that since the client is paying and since "the customer is always right," if the customer wants this information left out, it will be left out. Still others stand on their professionalism and refuse to change so much as a comma. You pay your money and you take your choice.

3. *Client wants proprietary information that you learned while employed with someone else.* This situation usually arises when you first become a consultant. A former competitor immediately contacts you about a potential engagement. It soon becomes clear, however, that he is hiring you not for what you can do but rather for what you know about your former employer. This situation can also come up when a potential client realizes that you have completed a consulting job for a competitor.

If it becomes clear that all the potential client wants is proprietary information, most consultants will refuse to get involved. You should also realize that unless you are a professional industrial spy—which, by the way, is illegal—a client who hires you for information you learned working for a competitor has every right to expect that you will give his proprietary information to someone else in the future. As a result, he will probably not hire you for any other purpose.

If a competitor wants to hire you for a job similar to one you did as a consultant in another company, it may be completely acceptable. "I heard about the great job that you did with the ABC Company; we'd like you to do the same thing for us," he may say. One fully ethical approach is to tell your potential client something like this: "I'd be happy to do this for you if I can get permission from the ABC Company. I don't think that I would be giving away any of their secrets if I did the same job for you. However, since you two are competitors, I would rather have their concurrence. Is that okay with you?"

4. *Client wants you to lie to his boss.* This usually involves a lower-level manager who wants you to lie to a manager at a higher level, or it could be the president of a company who wants you to lie to the board of directors or someone else outside the company. Some consultants have stated that it depends on the lie. A harmless "white lie" to protect someone's feelings, they might go along with. Others would not. Let's say that you are on assignment for the vice president of a company that is owned by the president, and as a part of this job you have to analyze the efficiency and effectiveness of all managers working for this vice president, one of whom happens to be the president's son. You rate the son as a very poor executive. When the vice president sees this report, he says something like this: "Look, the president of our company has a heart condition. If you report that his son is a very poor executive, it could easily upset him and may actually bring on a heart attack. How about toning this down a bit and saying that this executive is unsuited to his present position?" Many consultants would consider this a "white lie" and would go along with this request. Other consultants might take the position that this executive was very poor, and that this is what they intended to put in their report, heart attack or no.

Other lies are far more questionable in both their motives and the net result on the company officials, the firm's well-being, or even the general public. Some would say that agreeing to lie would depend on the effect that the lie would cause. Others say simply they would refuse to lie under any circumstance.

5. *You are a headhunter and a member of a client's firm wants you to recruit him.* This situation again demonstrates that what might be ethical under some circumstances is totally unethical under others. To honor this request is unethical for any headhunter. Under no conditions can a headhunter recruit from his client's firm, and no ethical headhunter would even consider it. If a member of a client's firm wanted you to recruit him, the only ethical thing that you could do is first seek approval from this individual's boss.

6. *Client wants you to bill for greater or lesser than the actual amount.* This can involve the law as well as ethics. And you can be certain that the

IRS would take a very dim view of this suggestion. But, aside from its possible legal connotations, it is also a lie. Would you do it or would you not?

All these are typical problems, and you will see many more in your practice. In all cases, only you can decide on the action to take. Some otherwise unethical practices are often considered ethical because of the nature of the work accomplished. These would probably include the marketing research and headhunting situations noted earlier, which are acceptable in their professions but certainly considered unethical for anyone else. The only analogy that I can think of is a military spy. The professional soldier is prohibited from spying. Spying is illegal. Yet, for a spy, spying is ethical.

More than 20 years ago a young Air Force lieutenant was ordered by a superior officer to falsify a report in order to make a score from a simulated aircraft attack appear better than it actually was. This lieutenant faced a serious moral and ethical dilemma; it appeared that his future career in the Air Force hinged on an outright lie. Despite considerable pressure, this lieutenant resisted and refused to lie. The threat of punitive action was never carried out, and he had an outstanding career right up until the time he left the Air Force. Today, this lieutenant has major responsibilities outside of the government that have little to do with flying. He rates his success in entirely different activities in no small part to this instance when he decided who he was and how he would live his life.

Ethical questions are rarely simple and rarely easy to resolve. Frequently, it's not merely a question of lying, cheating, or stealing, but of doing either the greater good or the lesser evil. Whatever you do, you must be able to respect yourself in the future, or you will be useless to your clients and to yourself.

10
MAKING PROFESSIONAL PRESENTATIONS

The success of a consultant engagement is based not only on actually doing the assignment professionally, but also on your ability to present the results of your work to your client. This chapter covers the important skills and techniques of presentations. I will show you five keys to presentation success.

OBJECTIVES OF PRESENTATIONS

With a presentation, you want to inform your client of the results of the assignment, to make recommendations that will benefit your client, and to confirm that you have done a good job so that you will be retained in the future. Each of these objectives is, in its own way, important.

If you don't take the time to build a case for your recommendations, explaining what has happened during the engagement, your client is less likely to accept your recommendations. Your client wants to know how you arrived at the conclusions that led to these recommendations, and why you used one methodology over others. If you ran into problems, your client also wants to know what these problems were and what assumptions you had to make. If there were changes to the original contract, even though prior approval has already been given, you should restate them, both to remind your client of these changes and to inform others.

Either the quality of the work that you have done or the recommendations you have made for action are the bottom line of the consulting engagement. It's results that you are actually getting paid for. Without them, although the engagement might make an interesting case study, it would be of no benefit to your client.

Confirming that you have done a good job so that you will be retained in the future is also important. If you've done a good job, you deserve recognition for it. You can do this only by convincing your client through your presentation. If you do it properly, your client will come away from the consulting engagement looking good, and you will be retained again: furthermore, you will get referrals to additional clients who would like you to duplicate your success for them.

FIVE KEYS TO A SUCCESSFUL PRESENTATION

Every successful presentation has five essential components. These are:

1. Professionalism
2. Enthusiasm
3. Organization
4. Practice
5. Visual aids

Let's look at each in turn.

Professionalism

The quality of professionalism must be evident throughout your presentation. It is demonstrated by your dress and personal appearance; the quality of the visual aids you use; your demeanor; your preparation; and your delivery.

If you show up for a presentation wearing a suit that needs pressing or clothes that are not appropriate for the occasion, you will not be perceived as a professional.

If there are typographical or grammatical mistakes in your visual aids, or if the lettering is sloppy, this also will not be perceived as professional.

If the way you handle yourself during the presentation indicates that you are unsure of yourself or defensive, or that you do not know what you are talking about, you will not be perceived as a professional.

If things go wrong during your presentation because of an obvious lack of preparation, again, you will not be perceived as a professional.

But if your presentation is clear and well-organized, if it goes like clockwork and you are prepared to answer all questions asked, if your appearance matches your performance—then your professionalism will be obvious.

Enthusiasm

Enthusiasm, the second key to a successful presentation, is absolutely crucial. If you do nothing else, be enthusiastic. If you are not enthusiastic about what you did, I guarantee you that your client will not be enthusiastic either. In my opinion, enthusiasm is the most important secret of making a good presentation.

What should you do if you really are not enthusiastic? First of all, it is very difficult for me to believe that you could ever become a good consultant and *not* be enthusiastic about what you are doing. But if, for whatever reason, you really are not enthusiastic about this particular assignment, there is only one thing you can do—*pretend*. Whenever I tell my senior students about the absolute necessity of enthusiasm, I always tell them the story of General George S. Patton, Jr., one of the most successful generals of World War II. He won battles *and* saved the lives of his men by motivating them to do their very best. And he did this by becoming a consummate actor.

I have read Patton's published diaries, which go back as far as the turn of the century when Patton was a cadet at West Point. During World War I when still in his 20s, he was a colonel in command of the U.S. Army's first tank corps. Patton wrote his wife regularly, and these letters were published with the diaries. In one letter Patton says, "Every day I practice in front of a mirror looking mean." Can you imagine that? A hard-boiled colonel of the American Army practicing in front of a mirror looking mean? But Patton did this for a reason. He knew that his ability to motivate his men—sometimes by joking, sometimes by intimidation—could win battles and could save lives. And so he made himself become a great actor.

If Patton could act to save lives and win battles, then you can act, and act enthusiastically, to make a successful consultant presentation. Remember, you *must* do this. It is not an option. It is the most important secret of success in presenting. You must be enthusiastic, and you must show this enthusiasm to your client audience. I promise you that the enthusiasm, even though self-generated, will come through, and will help make your presentation successful.

Organization

You can't just stand up and speak without having thought ahead of time what you are going to say. Even a terrific off-the-cuff speaker would get into trouble if he made consultant presentations that way. If you try it, invariably certain facts will be left out, and then your presentation will not be as clear and logical as it must be. If you are questioned because of this lack of clarity, the pressure on you will increase and your difficulties will become even greater.

Proper organization of your presentation ahead of time will save you many problems once you are face to face with your client. Fortunately, we already have the ingredients of our presentation from work we did in earlier chapters, including material from the contract, the proposal, and even our initial interview. So we can organize the facts of the engagement and present them to the client in a clear and logical manner, using this outline:

1. Background of the consulting assignment and the problem to be solved.

2. Statement of the project objectives.
3. Methodologies used to do the assignment, along with alternative methodologies and reasons why they were rejected.
4. Problems encountered during the engagement and how each was handled.
5. The results or conclusions stemming from this engagement.
6. Specific recommendations to the client on what he should do as a result of the work you have done, not excluding additional work that must be done by you or someone else in the future.

Practice

Practice does not mean that you must read your report aloud or that you must memorize anything. In fact, the contrary is true. Reading will make the presentation boring and stilted. It is not natural.

The same is true of memorization. Even if you have the ability to memorize quickly, I do not recommend using it in a consulting presentation. First, the time spent in memorization can be better used in getting your presentation together. Second, there is always a chance that under the pressures of the situation your timing and memory may be thrown off by a question asked out of turn or a discussion initiated by your client.

I learned this lesson myself the hard way. As a young Air Force officer flying B-52s out of Altus, Oklahoma, I was extremely interested in navigation. On one occasion the Texas Math and Science Teachers Association contacted my Wing commander to ask if there was someone who could travel to its annual meeting in Wichita Falls and speak for about an hour on a subject of interest to the members. The Wing commander asked me, and, since I had waited for a chance to do research in space navigation, I jumped at the chance. Using notes collected over several months, I wrote a terrific one-hour presentation (at least I thought it was terrific, and it must have been reasonably good, because it was later published by a national magazine). I was also given the opportunity to have excellent artwork prepared into 35mm slides. I felt that I had the very best support possible. But I made one mistake—I memorized every single word in that one-hour presentation. I even knew where to pause for the commas! When the time came, I went down to Wichita Falls and, in full uniform, looked out at nearly 300 math and science teachers. I had been a junior high school student in that very same city, and seeing so many teachers looking at me immediately had its effect. I forgot parts of my presentation, became flustered, and eventually had to read it word for word. What a failure! But it taught me a valuable lesson, and never since then have I memorized anything, even though I am frequently a guest speaker for many different organizations. Do not repeat my mistake. Do not memorize, and do not read anything.

If you don't read and you don't memorize, how are you supposed to make your presentation? Very easily. Once you have your material organized, you can use either 3″ × 5″ file cards or visual aids to help you discuss each point. You might have one card that says "background of the consulting assignment and the problem." You would then simply look up and talk to your audience about this background. If there are any important statistics that you do not wish to leave out, you would put them sequentially on other cards. Other main ideas are also on sequential cards. But you should write no more than one sentence on each card. The idea is not to read what is written on each card, but rather to talk about that one sentence. If you are using visual aids, they could display the key sentence or statistics to remind you of what you are going to talk about at that particular time.

Controlling Time

It is extremely important as a part of your practice to control the time available for your presentation. If your client says she wants a one-hour presentation, make it a one-hour presentation. If she wants 30 minutes, make it that. Do not under any circumstances extend your presentation unless requested to do so. That is disaster. Let me tell you two stories to prove my point.

I was once associated with a major aerospace company that was bidding on a multibillion-dollar contract for the government. On one of the reviews, representatives of the government visited our organization for a four-hour briefing by our engineers. These engineers lost control of the time and went well over the limit requested by the customer. Despite frantic signals from company employees, they completed their presentation more than an hour and a half late. The customers remained the extra hour and a half without complaint, but they missed their return flights. And while I would not say this was the only reason that the large contract was lost, it was certainly a factor.

Failing to control time will almost always get you into trouble. Some years ago I was on a search committee to find a new professor for our department at the university. The procedure in academia is somewhat different than in industry, and in many hirings the professor must be voted on and accepted by the department before the university can make an offer. Usually a candidate for faculty membership must not only interview with many department members, but must make a formal presentation to the department sitting as a group. On this occasion, the candidate, who had only recently obtained his PhD, was asked to make a 20-minute presentation about the research for his dissertation. The time limit was necessary because many faculty members had other meetings to attend. The candidate had graduated from an excellent university, and prior to his visit most of the members had decided to vote for his hiring based solely on his background and experience. During the visit, the individual interviews seemed to be going fairly well. The presentation was the final obstacle before the department voted on his hiring. He began his presentation. Five minutes passed. Ten minutes passed. Fifteen minutes passed. Twenty minutes came and went. The presentation continued on and on. The entire department was restless; other meetings were late. Individuals slipped out one after the other. Finally, after 45 minutes, the candidate concluded. By then, a receptive faculty eager to hire him no longer existed. The faculty did eventually vote to hire, but only for a one-year appointment. In fact, it was two years before this individual was finally granted the permanent position that he all but had even before his visit. It is no exaggeration to say that failure to control time for 25 additional minutes cost two years of promotion, pay, and other benefits.

Never think that time control is a small item—it is essential.

The Practice Sequence

Here's the practice sequence I use: First I note the time available and outline the presentation using the organizational structure indicated earlier. I write this information on 3″ × 5″ file cards. I then go through the presentation once, using the cards. In this run-through I change the cards, add facts, if required, and delete or change others if they don't seem to fit. I watch my time closely as I make this presentation to myself, and make adjustments, through insertion or deletion of material, so that my presentation is several minutes less than the time I have been allotted.

If there are several presenters, I insist that we practice together. Some consultants simply divide the available time and develop separate presentations, but I have found that such a presentation doesn't quite fit together when done before the client. Further, frequently one or more of the presenters will exceed the amount of time allotted, and the total presentation runs much longer than anticipated.

I practice at first very informally, perhaps just sitting around a table or in a room by myself or with the other presenters. I do this several times until I am confident of the overall structure and the time. Now I also know what visual aids I will need and can have them made.

The Formal Practice Presentation

The formal practice presentation is done as if it were real. In fact, I insist upon doing it in front of someone who can give me feedback. Usually this is my wife, but it has also been a colleague or someone else who is not involved in the presentation itself. You must present it to an outsider who is not a part of the consultant presentation team.

Live Demonstration

If there is some demonstration to be done as a part of the presentation, I insist upon a practice live demonstration. This is essential to make sure it fits into the time and also that the results of the demonstration are as anticipated. Live demonstrations are essential to ensure that the actual presentation before your client goes correctly. You will find that at actual presentations everything that can go wrong will go wrong. Therefore you must anticipate and eliminate potential problems before they actually happen.

Let me give you an example of how important this can be. Some years ago I was attending an annual meeting of the Survival and Flight Equipment Association, an organization of mixed industry, military, and civilian airline personnel who develop and manufacture life-support equipment for people who fly. A project manager from the Navy was making a very interesting presentation on a very important piece of equipment.

A Navy flier has special problems because he flies over the sea. If he must eject from his aircraft, he hits the water. He must climb into a small life raft while weighted down with survival gear, boots, helmet, etc. This is difficult enough even on a calm sea, but it is almost impossible if the parachute is still attached to him, since even the slightest wind will drag the chute. If the open chute fills with water, it can drag the aviator straight to the bottom. So the approved procedure is to use a quick-release, attached to the harness, to get rid of the parachute just as the aviator's boots touch the water. The problem with this procedure is that it is very difficult to judge height over a flat surface like the ocean, and it's even more difficult in the dark under the pressure of emergency conditions. As a result, some aviators who thought they were just about to touch the water were actually 100 feet or more in the air. Jettisoning the chute at that height is clearly not recommended. The Navy's solution was highly innovative as well as effective. A small explosive squib in the parachute harness separated the chute from the harness on contact with water; the water completed an electrical contact. Thus, when the aviator entered the water, the parachute would be blown away from him automatically.

Now you may be thinking, That's just fine for the ocean water, but what if a pilot must eject through a rain shower? Does this mean the apparatus will become wet and that the aviator will be dropped thousands of feet? The Navy had anticipated this problem. The device would work only in sea water, which has a high salt content.

The Navy project manager explained all this in a most interesting fashion and finally came to the most dramatic point of the presentation. He himself donned a parachute. While he could not submerge his whole body, he had two live wires leading to the squib and had a glass of sea water before him. He then described in vivid terms exactly what would happen. He would take the two wires and thrust them into the sea water. We would see a flash and hear a loud bang, he said, and the parachute would be separated from the harness instantly. The entire audience waited in great anticipation; several people stuck their fingers in their ears. Knowing that he had everyone's attention, the presenter, with the parachute strapped tightly to his body, took the two wires and jammed them into the sea water. Nothing happened. At first there were smirks, then scattered laughter spread throughout the room. This presenter—who had otherwise made a perfect presentation—took the harness off and discovered that someone had failed to replace the electrical batteries.

Let this teach you the lesson that it taught me. Always prepare for any live demonstrations by actually doing the full demonstration yourself. Don't assume that something will work as planned. Actually do the demonstration as a part of your practice.

Visual Aids

Visual aids are also essential to a good presentation. In general, you have four options for good visual aids:

1. Flip charts
2. Overhead transparencies
3. 35mm slides
4. Handouts

Flip Charts

Flip charts are large charts connected at the top that are flipped over as each one is used. The main advantage of flip charts is that they don't require any type of projector. However, since they are large, they are sometimes difficult to transport. And depending on the size of your audience, you may not be able to make the lettering large enough to be seen by everyone in the room.

Overhead Transparencies

Overhead transparencies require the use of an overhead projector. Transparencies themselves usually have a viewing area of approximately 8½ × 11 inches. Machines are available today to make these transparencies instantly without the use of photographic equipment. If you have a typewriter with large letters and have access to a transparency reproduction machine, you can make visuals fairly rapidly. If not, they can be done at many printing and art shops. Transparencies themselves are fairly easy to carry around. They are not as small as 35mm slides but they are easier to use than slides and much easier to transport than flip charts. They can, however, be expensive, as much as several dollars each. And of course, they require the use of the special projector already mentioned.

35mm Slides

Slides are very easy to transport. They do require the use of a slide projector, however, and they can be expensive. As is sometimes the case with transparencies, slides require additional lead time, usually a week or so.

Handouts

Handouts can be typed on a piece of paper and reproduced through one of the many photographic reproduction processes, at a few cents per page. They can be used for either small or large groups, and the expense depends on the number that must be reproduced. You can make the handouts yourself, and they can be prepared at the last minute, without a long lead time, both of which factors are important. For smaller groups it is fairly easy to carry around the handouts with you. However, for a large group and a large handout, this becomes cumbersome and expensive. One additional disadvantage is that your audience may tend to read ahead of you; if you have some dramatic point to make, it could be spoiled by your audience getting there first.

Whatever option you select in visual aids, make sure you keep these points in mind:

1. *Use big type*. The print must be large enough to be visible. If your visual aids cannot be read, you might as well not use them.

2. *Keep it simple*. Don't put too much information on a single slide, transparency, chart, or page of a handout. The information should only be keys to remind you of your major points and to reinforce these major points with your audience. Entire explanations, facts, figures, and so forth

can be included as an appendix to your written report. If you put too much information on a single visual, you will only confuse your audience.

3. *Allow lots of lead time.* While handouts can be changed fairly easily, flip charts, transparencies, and slides take longer. Plan to have them completed a couple of days before the presentation itself. Typographical errors are common, and they must be corrected before the presentation. Even a simple spelling error leaves the thought in your client's mind, "If he has made this error and allowed it to pass, what else has he screwed up?"

OVERCOMING STAGE FRIGHT

Every great presenter is a little apprehensive about making a presentation. If you weren't apprehensive, you would be indifferent and the presentation would be boring. So, a little bit of stage fright is fine. On the other hand, you do not want to be so apprehensive that you cannot make a smooth, forceful, and motivating presentation.

In order to overcome stage fright, I do two things. First, I accomplish at least two live rehearsals before other people. These are formal demonstrations to people not familiar with the presentation so that I can receive feedback and criticism on what I say. This criticism allows me to polish my presentation and often uncovers rough points I never thought about.

The second thing I do is something called creative visualization. Somehow I stumbled into this technique, and because it is a little strange, for many years I didn't tell too many people about it. Then, in the January 13, 1982, issue of *The Wall Street Journal* I read an article about it. A performance psychologist at Berkeley had found one reason why some people were superior performers. It was the trick of mental rehearsal, something top athletes have done for a long time. Top chief executives would visualize every aspect of what it would be like to have a successful presentation—sort of a deliberate daydreaming. A run-of-the-mill executive, this psychologist said, would organize his facts but not his psyche.

Thus, my creative visualization got official blessing from a performance psychologist and *The Wall Street Journal.* Believe me when I tell you the technique is simple. I like to do it the night before I make the presentation, just before I go to sleep. I'm lying there with nothing else to do; I go through my entire presentation, not memorizing it but going through it in my mind from start to finish, from the time I first enter the room until my conclusion. I visualize everything that happens, including standing up and shaking hands, describing the background to the assignment, the objectives of the project, the methods I used and why I chose them, the problems and how they were handled, the resulting conclusions, and the recommendations to my client. I even visualize questions that are asked and my answering them forcefully and correctly. I visualize smiles all the way around, knowing that I have made an excellent presentation and that everyone, including and especially the client who hired me, is happy with the excellent job I have done. I don't stop at doing this one time; I repeat the visualization episode several times. You can visualize an entire hour presentation in a few minutes, and then you can repeat it again and again.

To my way of thinking, this creative visualization technique offers several outstanding features. First, when you actually go to stand up to make the presentation, it doesn't feel new. You've done it dozens of times before. This takes the sting out of stage fright. Second, I believe that visualizing my presentation in a positive fashion, as a success, prepares me positively. I believe that my presentation will be successful, and therefore it is. I sense that my audience will be friendly to me, and therefore it is. I have confidence in my ability to answer questions because I have already seen myself doing these things.

In my years of using this creative visualization technique, it has never failed me. I strongly recommend that you try it too. The results will amaze you.

One variation I have heard about is called the split-focus technique. In this technique, you visualize the presentation while you are physically doing something else. You can practice the technique while working in the garden or taking a shower.

ANSWERING QUESTIONS

Many presenters fear answering questions more than anything else; yet research has shown that 85% of the questions asked during a presentation can actually be anticipated. Therefore, when I prepare myself for a presentation, I sit down and try to anticipate questions that members of my client's company are likely to ask me. I actually write them down. Some of the questions bring up items I feel should be included, so I modify my presentation accordingly. Others I just think I should be ready for, and so I simply think them through and write out the answers. If additional statistics or information is necessary to give a complete answer, I ensure I have this information available. In some cases I even go so far as to make up a special visual aid with the information, which I hold in readiness to use only if I am asked this question.

When I am actually asked a question, I always repeat it. This gives me additional time to think about the answer and at the same time it ensures that other members of the audience hear the question too.

The best way to answer is to first repeat the question, then state your answer, and then state why your answer is what it is—give supporting facts. I try never to be defensive about a question, even if it is asked in a belligerent tone of voice. In fact, remembering that the customer is always right, I try never to get into an argument with a client. This does not mean that I agree that the client is right if he is not. It simply means that I state the facts as I know them and if the client insists on arguing, I explain my position as tactfully as possible and move on to something else.

One important key to answering questions—in fact for your whole presentation—is to view the audience as friends and not adversaries. Do this even if the climate is political and some members of the audience can be expected to snipe at you. You can at least treat them as friendly snipers and not enemies out to demolish you.

The other point to watch out for is not to get into a long-winded answer. Try to make your answers short and to the point. Long-winded answers only fuzzy the issue, and may lead to more in-depth questioning.

If you follow all the above advice, you cannot fail to have an outstanding presentation. Not only will you receive accolades for it, but your advice will be respected and followed and will lead to further consulting assignments.

11
HOW TO RUN YOUR CONSULTING BUSINESS

No matter how excellent you are as a consultant, unless you are a good business manager you will not realize your full potential; your business could even go bankrupt because of your failure to sustain a profit. Therefore, this chapter is crucial. I will explain the various forms of business organization including proprietorships, partnerships, and corporations. I will include information on getting business licenses, resale permits, fictitious name registration, use of credit cards, stationery, business cards, insurance, and personal liability. I will also tell you about other important topics such as how to keep your overhead low, what expenses to anticipate, and what records you should maintain.

SELECTING THE LEGAL STRUCTURE FOR YOUR CONSULTING FIRM

There are several different structures recognized by law from which you can choose for your consulting practice. These are the sole proprietorship, the partnership, and the corporation. Each structure has its own advantages and disadvantages, and you should select the one that is most suitable for you.

The Sole Proprietorship

The sole proprietorship is a business structure for a firm that is owned by only one person. To establish a sole proprietorship, all you need to do is obtain whatever business licenses are required in your local area. This makes it the easiest of legal structures to set up. It is also the one most frequently used for many types of small businesses and certainly one that you should consider for your practice.

Advantages

The advantages of the sole proprietorship include the following:
1. *Ease and speed of formation*. With the sole proprietorship, there are

fewer formalities and legal requirements. Sometimes you need only visit your county clerk, fill out a simple form, and pay the license fee, which is generally $100 or less. In most cases there is no waiting period; you can satisfy all legal requirements the same day you make your visit.

2. *Reduced expense.* Because of the minimal legal requirements, the sole proprietorship can be set up without an attorney, so it is much less expensive than either a partnership or a corporation.

3. *Total control.* Since you have no partners and since it is not a corporation, complete control of the management of your firm is yours; as long as you fulfill the legal requirements, you run your business as you see fit. Other than your clients, you have no boss. You and the marketplace make all the decisions. This has the additional advantage of responsiveness: you can usually respond much more quickly to changes in the marketplace.

4. *Sole claim to profits.* Since you are the sole owner, you are not required to share your profits with anyone. The profits are yours, as are all the assets of the business.

Disadvantages

Disadvantages of the sole proprietorship include:

1. *Unlimited liability.* While you own all assets and are responsible for all decision-making in a sole proprietorship, you are also held to unlimited personal liability. This means that you are responsible for the full amount of business debts and judgments against your business. This could amount to more money than you have invested in your business. If your business fails with you owing money to various creditors, these debts could be collected from your personal assets. Of course there are various methods of reducing this risk, through proper insurance coverage, which I will discuss later in this chapter.

2. *No one to consult with.* Since in a sole proprietorship you are probably a one-person show, you are limited by your own skills, education, background, and capabilities. You may be able to get advice and counsel from friends, relatives, or business acquaintances, but no one is motivated by personal investment to give you this advice, nor will the giver suffer the consequences if the advice proves to be poor.

3. *Difficulty in absences.* Again, since there is only you, you will have to find someone to cover for you when you are sick or on vacation. Of course there are various ways around this limitation. You could agree to watch over the practice of some other consultant who works in the same area with the understanding that she will do the same for you when re-

quired. You could also pay someone to cover for you during your periods of absence. But no matter what solution you select, until you have employees working for you who can perform certain services for clients, it is a limitation that must be considered.

4. *Difficulties in raising capital.* Potential lenders see the sole proprietorship as represented essentially by one person. As a result, they feel the risk is greater than if there were more people involved, as in a partnership, or if you had a permanent legal identity such as a corporation.

The Partnership

Legally, the partnership can be entered into by simply acquiring a business license from your county clerk. However, unlike the sole proprietorship, I don't recommend that you attempt to do this by yourself; use the assistance of an attorney. Partnership definitions may vary in different states, and it is extremely important to document the obligation of each of the partners regarding investments, profits, and obligations with a partnership agreement. Such an agreement should typically cover the following aspects of the practice:

1. Absence and disability.
2. Arbitration.
3. Authority of individual partners in the conduct of the business.
4. Character of partners, including whether general or limited, active or silent.
5. Contributions by partners, both now and at a later time.
6. Dissolution of the practice if necessary.
7. Division of profits and losses.
8. Salary, including draws from the business during its growth state or at any period thereafter.
9. Duration of the agreement.
10. Managerial assignment within the firm.
11. Expenses and how they will be handled by each partner.
12. Name, purpose, and domicile of the partnership.
13. Performance by partners.
14. Records and methods of accounting.
15. Release of debts.
16. Required acts and prohibited acts.
17. Rights of continuing partner.
18. Sale of partnership interest.
19. Separate debts.
20. Settlement of disputes.

How a Partnership Differs from a Sole Proprietorship

It is important to understand the elements that differentiate a partnership from a sole proprietorship. A partnership features:

1. Co-ownership of the assets
2. Limited life of the partnership
3. Mutual agency
4. Share in management
5. Share in partnership profits
6. Unlimited liability of at least one partner

Advantages

There are advantages of the partnership, including the following:

1. *Ease and speed of formation.* Like the sole proprietorship, it is fairly easy and quick to establish a consulting business using the partnership structure.

2. *Access to additional capital.* In a sole proprietorship the initial capital must come from your personal funds or loans from other sources. In the case of a partnership, you have at least one other source of additional capital for your consulting practice.

3. *Assistance in decision-making.* It is said that two heads are better than one. With a partnership you have at least one other person to help you analyze the various situations that you may come across in the management of the business, and to conduct the consulting work itself.

4. *Vacation and sickness stability.* When you have a partner, it's much easier to take a vacation or to have someone else handle clients when you are ill. Partners can cover for each other.

Disadvantages

Like all other structures of business, there are disadvantages with the partnership, and some of them are severe. In fact, many attorneys recommend against a partnership because of potential problems later on. However, it should also be noted that many law firms themselves are organized as partnerships.

1. *Liability for actions of partners.* All partners are bound by the actions of any one partner, and under normal circumstances you are liable for the actions and commitments of any partner. Thus, a single partner can expend resources or make business commitments, and all partners are liable whether or not they agree.

2. *Potential organizational disputes.* Organizations are made up of human beings. As a result, partners, especially equal partners, disagree. Even friends may find themselves at loggerheads if it is not clearly decided ahead of time, and in writing, who is the president, who the chief executive officer, who the vice president, and so on. It has been said that for this reason, partnerships have all the disadvantages of a marriage with none of the advantages.

3. *Difficulty in obtaining capital.* Like a sole proprietorship, a partnership may be viewed as less stable than a corporation. As a result, in comparison to a corporation, it is relatively more difficult to raise capital when and if needed.

The Corporation

Unlike a sole proprietorship or a partnership, a corporation is a legal entity separate and distinct from its owner. Also unlike the other two, corporations cannot be viewed as simple organizational structures. It is possible to set up a corporation without the aid of an attorney, but I don't recommend it. The reason is that state laws on corporations differ, and there are many tradeoffs for the state you operate in that should be explained by an attorney. Also, corporations that do business in more than one state must comply with the federal laws on interstate commerce and with the laws of the various states, which vary considerably. Further, you can limit yourself severely and may actually be in violation of the law if you deviate from the purpose of the corporation as set forth when you incorporate. Again, attorneys can be of great help here; in my experience the basic forms found in books telling you how to form your own corporation can lead to problems later on down the road.

Advantages

The major advantages of forming a corporation are as follows:

1. *Limited liability.* As a corporation, your liability is limited to the amount of your investment in the business. This protects you from creditors or judgments against you, since you can lose only what you have invested and not your personal holdings outside of the business. However, the limited liability concept does *not* apply to corporations that offer professional services, and it is entirely possible that some consultancies might fall into that category.

2. *Income tax advantages.* Because tax laws change frequently, you should always check with an accountant. Currently the maximum rate of federal income tax on corporations is 46% of the net profits, while the maximum personal income tax is currently 50% (in the past it has been as

high as 90%). So there may be some tax advantages to you with a corporate structure. If you are incorporated, the money left in the corporation, which is used to help the firm grow (and is *not* paid out to shareholders), will be taxed only at the lower corporation tax rate. If you are not incorporated, all your profit will be taxed at the personal income tax rate, which may well be higher. If you sell the stock of the firm at some time in the future, you would qualify for capital gains treatment, which would result in lower taxes than if the profits were treated as ordinary income. Consult your accountant for current tax information and advice.

3. *Relative ease in obtaining capital.* Many consulting firms need capital at one time or another for expansion or other purposes. Lenders of all types are usually more willing to make loans to an organization with a more permanent legal entity, such as a corporation, than either of the other two basic types of structures. However, note that many banks may require the officer or officers of a small corporation to personally cosign loans.

4. *Additional human resources.* A board of directors is required for a corporation. As long as qualified board members are appointed, more help will be available to you as an integral part of the business than would be the case with either a partnership or a sole proprietorship. It should also be noted, however, that a one-person corporation is in the same boat as a sole proprietorship—should the owner be absent, no one will be there to cover.

5. *Credibility to clients and the industry.* A corporation, because of its permanent legal status, generally has more credibility with potential clients. Admittedly, at some point in the lifetime of your firm this becomes a very minor advantage, since your firm's reputation, whether incorporated or not, will be the primary factor. But at the start, incorporation could be of some importance.

Disadvantages

Just as with the other business structures, there are disadvantages to the corporation. These include the following:

1. *Additional paperwork and government regulations.* There are a fair amount of paperwork and many more regulations associated with the corporation than with either of the other two.

2. *Reduced control.* In a corporation you must have a board of directors. There will be additional local, state, and federal government regulations to contend with. This tends to restrict business activities much more than with the simpler types of business structures. Also, the corporation

cannot diverge from its mission statement without an amendment to its corporate charter.

3. *Expense in formation.* The corporate structure is the most expensive to form, because of the need to use an attorney. It is also slower to set up.

4. *Taxes.* Depending upon your situation and the profits in your business, you could end up paying more taxes than otherwise, because of double taxation. Any money you take out of the business in dividends is taxed a second time as personal income. In addition, if your salary is declared unreasonably high by the IRS, a portion of your salary may be termed a dividend and taxed again as well.

5. *Inability to take losses as deductions.* If you lose money in your business with either a partnership or a sole proprietorship, you will be able to take these losses as deductions for personal income tax purposes (this is an advantage of a partnership or a sole proprietorship). With a corporation, losses sustained in the current year cannot be used to reduce other personal income. However, a corporation's loss may be carried forward or back to reduce another year's income. There is an exception in dealing with corporation losses; it involves setting up a special type of corporation. You should discuss this possibility with your accountant or attorney.

OTHER LEGAL NECESSITIES

Once you decide on a form of business structure, you still have a few other legal details to take care of.

Obtaining a Business License

As noted earlier, unless you incorporate, you generally will need only a local business license, either a municipal or county license, or both. The license may require that you conform to certain zoning laws and building codes, and meet other regulations set forth by local health, fire, or police departments. However, usually these restrictions are minimal and fairly easily met in the case of a consulting practice. Certain permits may be required for certain types of consultancies or activities that are considered hazardous or in some other way detrimental to the community. But if you are required to obtain such a permit, you will be informed when you purchase the business license. Again, for a consulting practice, usually this will not be required.

Some states require licensing for certain occupations, and this may affect certain types of consulting practices. Again, if this is the case, you will be informed when you get your local business license. For example, most states require personnel recruiters who place job applicants to be licensed. For complete information contact your state department of commerce.

There are also federal licensing requirements for some businesses that could affect certain types of consulting, such as an investment advisory service. Again, you will usually be informed if you need an additional license when you get your local business license. But to be absolutely certain, contact the U.S. Department of Commerce, which can be found under the U.S. Government listing in your local telephone directory.

The Resale Permit

If your state has a sales tax, it also has a state board to control and collect the tax. Usually this board will allow you to secure a resale permit.

The resale permit has two purposes. First, it assigns you duties as an agent of the state in the collection of taxes for products subject to sales tax. Second, it allows you to purchase items you intend to resell to someone else without paying the tax yourself. In purchasing such products from a vendor, you must give your resale permit number, or otherwise you must pay the tax. If a fee is required to obtain a resale permit, the agency involved will inform you at the time you apply for it. Frequently, this agency requires security from you in the form of a cash deposit against the payment of future state tax on the products that you will sell. This amount can be sizable, as much as several thousand dollars in some states. If you fail to pay any sales tax due, the state can deduct this amount from your deposit. Thus, they are protected even if you go bankrupt. Bear in mind that in most states, there is no sales tax on professional services, only on the sale, rental, and repair of tangible personal property. Check your local state regulations.

It is definitely not to your advantage to tie up several thousand dollars of your hard-earned cash merely to satisfy a security deposit for a resale permit. However, the amount of money required—if any—depends on the information you provide at the time you obtain the resale permit. In some cases, where the deposit is high, installment payment arrangements can be made. Minimum requirements are usually determined when certain conditions are met. These situations include: if you own your home and have substantial equity in it; if the estimated monthly expenses of your consulting practice are low; if your estimated monthly sales are low; if you are presently employed and your business activities are part-time; if you have no employees other than yourself; and if you have only one place of business. As I said before, services are usually not taxed, only products.

But if products are part of your business or an adjunct to your consulting practice, you should obtain a resale permit if there is a state tax in your state.

Fictitious Name Registration

Fictitious name registration is required if you use any name in your practice other than your own. If you use a business name that includes names other than yours or your partners', or that implies the existence of additional partners, or indeed implies anything that your practice is not, you will need fictitious name registration. Thus, "James A. Smith" is a perfectly acceptable business name that does not require fictitious name registration as long as your name is actually James A. Smith. However, "James A. Smith and Associates" requires fictitious name registration. There are some fictitious names that you usually cannot use at all. You cannot, for example, call yourself "a university," a "research center," or other descriptions that imply a nonprofit corporation unless you are one. Most states will prohibit you from using the title "Doctor," "Reverend," or "Professor" unless you meet certain legal requirements. But other than these types of restrictions, most "doing business as" names are acceptable, as long as you obtain the proper registration. Interestingly, consulting firms may use fictitious name registration; law and CPA firms may not.

Fictitious name registration is usually very easy; it should not be considered a major problem in setting up your consulting practice. First, find out the law in your state by contacting someone such as the county clerk. Typically there is a small registration fee of less than $50 and another small fee, perhaps $30 to $50, for publication of your registration in a general circulation newspaper distributed in the area in which you intend to do business. Once publication is accomplished, you file the affidavit with your county clerk's office. In many cases the newspapers can handle the entire matter for you. The form is simple, and filling it out will take you only a few minutes. Many states will allow you to obtain more than one fictitious name on the form. For some types of consulting practices, this could be useful; it will allow you to test certain products under names other than your client's or the regular business name of your practice. Then, if the product fails in the marketplace, it will have no effect on either your or your client's image.

Fictitious name registration is in force for a predetermined fixed period, which varies by state; five years is typical. In many cases newspapers will write you ahead of time offering to handle the whole renewal business for you. In this way they secure publication of the form in their newspaper.

CLIENTS' USE OF CREDIT CARDS

Credit cards, such as Visa and MasterCard, are becoming increasingly useful for the professional consulting practice. In fact, many other professionals, such as doctors and dentists, may accept credit cards from their patients or clients today. Accepting credit cards has two major benefits for you. First, it adds additional credibility. Firms or individuals that have not done business with you before will recognize the Visa or MasterCard name, and will realize that those agencies investigated you before allowing you to use their services. Second, the consumer credit company will provide credit to your clients and will collect the money for you. Thus, several thousand dollars in consulting fees can be billed and paid over a period of time without you being the collection agency. Of course, there is a disadvantage to using consumer credit companies: you will pay the company a certain percentage of each billing. Usually, the higher your credit card sales, the lower the percentage the consumer credit company will charge. The percentage involved is generally about 4% of the sale.

STATIONERY AND BUSINESS CARDS

It's extremely important that you get the highest-quality business cards and stationery that you possibly can. These items represent you to your clientele and communicate a message about the type of firm you are. Get the most expensive you can afford. Your stationery should have at least 25% rag content, and your name should be engraved. The raised print has a classic appearance. (A less expensive way to achieve this raised look is a process known as thermography.) The same is true of your business cards. If a logo is used, it should be simple and representative of the type of consulting you do. "High-class professional" is what you want your stationery and business cards to say.

INSURANCE AND PERSONAL LIABILITY

As a consultant, you face certain risks, some of which you can insure against and some of which you cannot. For example, changes in economic and business conditions, the marketplace, or technology cannot be insured against. Any of these can change and hurt your business. However, other types of risks can be transferred through insurance. These include bad debts caused when subcontractors or clients go bankrupt, disasters caused by weather or fire, theft, liabilities from negligence and other actions, and death or disability of key company executives. You should think of insurance as a form of risk management. Do your risk managing in a four-step process.

1. *Identify* the risks to which your consulting practice will be subjected.
2. *Evaluate* the probability of occurrence of each risk. Also list the cost to you should this event occur and the cost of insurance protecting you against the risk.
3. *Choose* the best way to allow for each risk, whether to accept all or part of the risk, or to transfer the risk through insurance.
4. *Control* the risk by implementing what you select as the best method.

The services of direct writers are helpful in the risk-assessment process. A direct writer is a commissioned employee of the insurer; the business that he or she writes belongs to the insurance company. An agent, on the other hand, is an independent business person like yourself who has negotiated with the insurer to represent the insurer for a given territory. The agent is also compensated on a commission basis.

There are advantages in both cases. An independent agent may represent many different insurers, and so would be able to offer you a wider choice of coverages. Also, because the independent agent deals with these many different types, he or she may have a greater knowledge in the overall field than a direct writer whose experience is limited to the employer company. However, direct writers may cost less since their commission is less than that of the independent agent. Also, direct writers become specialists in their line, with in-depth knowledge and experience. This means that for a certain type of insurance of particular importance to you, this seller may know the finer details of the risk you are attempting to manage.

To locate direct writers or agents, consult your phone book or friends or acquaintances in business.

Insurance Checklist

A valuable checklist on insurance for small businesses was developed by Mark R. Greene, Distinguished Professor of Insurance at the University of Georgia. It will help you establish your risk-management program; if you already have insurance, it can help you discover areas in your insurance program that can be improved with reduced cost and increased effectiveness. It also serves as a guide on whom to talk with when dealing with your insurance agent, broker, or other insurance contacts. You can order the *Insurance Checklist for Small Businesses* from the Small Business Administration, 1441 L Street NW, Washington, D.C. 20416.

KEEPING OVERHEAD LOW

One of the most important pieces of advice that I can give to you in managing your consulting practice is to maintain a low overhead. This means keeping costs that do not directly contribute to each and every project or to marketing to the absolute minimum. Many new consultants feel, for example, that they must have a fancy office at a prestigious address. If an address is indeed important to your success, you can usually rent a maildrop in that important neighborhood. But usually this is not really an important factor in your being hired as a consultant. The fact is, most clients won't come to your office; usually you'll go to theirs.

Many years ago, when I was working for another company as director of research and development, I interviewed an individual who told me the following sad tale. He and several other senior executives in a major aerospace company resigned to form their own consulting practice. Each invested enough money to last many months—they thought. Coming from a large company in which each had had an expensive office, furniture, and a personal secretary, these new consultants found it impossible to control spending for what they considered minimum requirements. They acquired expensive offices in a high-rent area, and outfitted them with rich mahogany paneling and thick, luxurious rugs. But that rich image didn't save this fledgling consulting firm from bankruptcy; in a few weeks their money was depleted. On the other hand, I am acquainted with a wealthy search consultant who did a half a million dollars in billing his first year, out of his home. As his partner told me, he did hundreds of thousands of dollars in billings in his pajamas, but neither his clients nor the executives he placed ever knew.

Remember, at first you don't even need a secretary, only typing services. What you definitely don't need is a secretary sitting around with nothing to do except contribute to your ego.

For most consulting practices, it is better to consider a home office to start with, especially if you are beginning part-time. A home office is usually completely satisfactory. In my many years of consulting, I can count on one hand the number of times clients have visited the office that I maintain in my home. It happens usually if the client too is in a start-up situation and thus has no office for me to go to. Occasionally the pressure of time will prevent you from traveling, and your client will come to you. In one case, I had a multimillion-dollar accountant as a client; he calculated that since my billing rates were higher than his, it was less expensive if he did the traveling to my office rather than the other way around.

The Telephone

To keep overhead low and yet maintain a business telephone without a secretary, you have two alternatives. One is a telephone answering service; the second is to buy or rent a telephone-answering machine. Again, there are tradeoffs to be made, advantages and disadvantages to both. The telephone-answering machine is very inexpensive; a good, professional-quality machine can be had for between $100 and $200. The disadvantage is that some potential clients simply will not leave a message on an answering machine. However, I believe if your answering message is tactfully worded and if you promise to get back with the caller soon, you have the greatest probability of getting the message that you need to continue the business relationship.

Even though an answering service may cost more, it may not be as good. Some operators of an answering service are rude and inconsiderate, and will leave your caller on hold for long periods of time. This can be worse than a machine, where at least you control the friendliness and professionalism of the voice doing the answering. If you do use an answering service, I would recommend checking on it periodically to ensure that the operator has the highest standards of professionalism and is not losing clients through rudeness or incompetence.

Should you have a special business phone for the home? Maybe not. Business telephones are usually more expensive than personal telephones. It's true that the business telephone does entitle you to a special listing in the Yellow Pages, and if you want a special advertisement, as discussed in an earlier chapter, you will need a business telephone in order to get one. However, another quirk in many telephone systems is that they will charge you more to connect a business telephone than a personal telephone. Yet you can have a personal telephone converted to the business telephone at little or no extra charge. If your practice is listed under your real name, and you don't need the Yellow Pages listing as a consultant, it makes little sense to obtain a special business telephone—as defined by telephone companies. There is nothing wrong with having a telephone company install an additional personal phone that you call a "business telephone." As long as you use it for totally business purposes, it should be deductible for tax purposes. If it is listed on your business card and your stationery, as far as your clients know, it is your business telephone.

Anticipating Expenses

One of the biggest mistakes new consultants make is failure to anticipate expenses. Recognize ahead of time that certain expenses will be necessary to set up and run your consulting practice as a business. Plan ahead for these expenses when you estimate what being in business will cost. Typical consulting expenses may include:

Water, electricity, and gas

Office supplies

Postage

Auto expenses

Telephone

Travel other than by automobile

Promotional material, including brochures

Entertainment

Income taxes

Subscriptions to professional journals

Memberships in professional and other associations

There will undoubtedly be additional expenses depending upon the type of consulting practice you do. Make sure that you forget nothing; anticipate them *before* you establish your practice.

NECESSARY RECORDS AND THEIR MAINTENANCE

Good records are necessary for several reasons. You'll need them for preparing tax returns, measuring of management effectiveness and efficiency, reducing material waste, and even obtaining loans. These are the essential records you should maintain:

1. Daily summary of income received. Figure 11–1 shows a sample form.
2. An expense journal (see the example in Figure 11–2) that lists your expense payments in chronological order.

Figure 11-1. Daily summary of income received.

Day/Date Item Sold or Service Performed	Amount	
Total amount received today		
Total amount received through yesterday		
Total amount received to date		

Figure 11-2. Expense journal.

Date	To Whom Paid	Purpose	Check Number	Amount	
		Total expenditures			

3. An expense ledger summary (see Figure 11–3) in which cash and check payments are totaled by category—for example, rent, wages, and advertising.
4. An inventory purchase journal (if product is in any way a part of your practice) that notes shipments received, accounts payable, and cash available for future purchases, as shown in Figure 11–4.
5. An employee compensation record, listing hours worked, pay rate, and deductions withheld for both part-time and full-time employees; see sample in Figure 11–5.
6. An accounts receivable ledger for outstanding invoices; Figure 11–6 shows a sample form.

TAX OBLIGATIONS

As the owner of a business, you are responsible for payment of federal, state, and local taxes. Because the federal taxes tend to be the most complex for new consultants, we'll look at them first. There are four basic types of federal taxes that you may run into: income taxes, Social Security taxes, excise taxes, and unemployment taxes. Let's look at each in more detail.

Income Taxes

The amount of federal taxes you owe will depend on the earnings of your company and on your company's legal structure, as we discussed earlier in the chapter.

If you have a sole proprietorship or partnership, your other income exemptions and nonbusiness deductions and credits will also be important factors. The tax formula used will generally be the same as for the individual taxpayer. The only difference is that you will file an additional form (Schedule C of Form 1040, Profit or Loss from a Business or Profession) that identifies items of expense and income connected to your consulting business. If your business is a partnership, the partnership files a business return (Form 1065) and you report only your share of the profit or loss on your personal return.

However, there is an important difference between being a sole proprietor or a partner, and being a salaried employee working for someone else. As a sole proprietor or a partner, you are required by law to pay federal income taxes and self-employment taxes *as the income is received.* You do this by filing a Declaration of Estimated Tax, Form 1040ES, on or before April 15 every year. This declaration is an estimate of the income and self-employment taxes you expect to owe on the basis of anticipated

Figure 11-3. Expense journal summary.

Purpose	Total This Period		Total Up to This Period		Total to Date	
Advertising						
Car and truck expense						
Commissions						
Contributions						
Delivery expense						
Dues and publications						
Employee benefit program						
Freight						
Insurance						
Interest						
Laundry and cleaning						
Legal and professional services						
Licenses						
Miscellaneous expense						
Office supplies						
Pension and profit sharing plan						
Postage						
Rent						
Repairs						
Selling expense						
Supplies						
Tax						
Telephone						
Traveling and entertainment						
Utilities						
Wages						
Totals						

Figure 11-4. Inventory purchase journal.

Date	Inventory Ordered Carried Forward	Shipment Received/Date	Accounts Payable	Cash Available for Future Purchases
		Totals		

income and exemptions. Actual payment of tax is made quarterly—April 15, June 15, September 15, and January 15 of the following year. With each payment, adjustments to your original estimate can be made. As the owner of a new consultant practice, you may be required to file a declaration on a date other than April 15 if your expected income or exemptions change during the year. For details of this, check with your local office of the Internal Revenue Service.

If you have a corporation, you must also pay income tax on its net profits separate from the amount taken out for salary, which is considered part of your personal income. Currently, tax rates on corporations are graduated as follows: For income under $25,000, the tax rate is 15%; as income increases, the rate may go as high as 46%.

The income tax return for a corporation is due on the fifteenth day of the third month following the end of each taxable year. (A corporation's tax year does not have to coincide with the calendar year.) Payment of corporate taxes is generally done quarterly.

Figure 11-5. Employee compensation record.

Name _____ Social Security No. _____

Date	Period Worked (hours, days, weeks, or months)	Wage Rate	Total Wages		Deductions					Net Paid	
					Soc. Sec.	Fed. Inc. Tax	State Inc. Tax				
	Totals										

Figure 11-6. Accounts receivable ledger (for consulting services billed but not yet paid).

Date	Customer/Client Name	Products/Services	Amount Owed	Payments Made/Date

In order to operate your business, it is extremely important that you have the necessary funds to pay your income taxes on time. Your accountant can help you work out a budget to allow for this. You can also use the worksheet in Figure 11–7, developed by the Small Business Administration.

Withholding Income Taxes

According to the law you must withhold federal income tax payments for your employees, if you have any. These payments are passed on to the government periodically. The process begins when you hire a new employee. Your new employee must sign a Form W–4, Employee's Withholding Allowance Certificate, listing any exemptions and additional withholding allowances claimed. The completed W–4 is your authority to withhold income tax in accordance with the current withholding tables issued by the IRS. If an employee fails to furnish a certificate, you are required to withhold taxes as if he or she were a single person with no exemptions. Before December 1 of each year, you should ask your employees to file new exemption certificates for the following year if there has been a change in their exemption status. At the end of each year you must furnish each employee copies of the Form W–2, Wage and Tax Statement. As you are aware if you have worked for someone else, the employees must file a copy of this with their income tax return. You, as the employer, must also furnish a copy of this Form W–2 to the IRS on or before February 28 of each year. For complete details, contact the office of the IRS in your area.

And don't forget to check with your state office to find out if you are responsible for withholding your employees' state income taxes as well.

Withholding Social Security Taxes

For Social Security taxes you must deduct 7.05% from each employee's wages and as employer you must match that sum. As a self-employed person you must also pay your own Social Security taxes, but at a rate of 11.8% (the gross tax rate of 14.1% less a built-in 2.3% credit). If your employee makes more than $39,600 a year, however, you deduct a flat rate of $2,791.80 and match that. If you make more than $39,600, you pay a flat fee of $4,672.80 (11.8% × $39,600).

Remitting Federal Taxes

Remitting federal taxes involves two steps: you must *report* the income and Social Security taxes you have withheld from the employee's pay and you must *deposit* the funds you withheld. Reporting withheld income and Social Security taxes is done on Form 941. (When it comes

Figure 11-7. Worksheet for meeting tax obligations.

Kind of Taxes	Due Date	Amount Due	Pay to	Date for Writing the Check
Federal Taxes				
Employee income taxes and Social Security taxes	____	____	____	____
	____	____	____	____
	____	____	____	____
	____	____	____	____
Excise Taxes	____	____	____	____
Owner–manager's and/or corporation's income taxes	____	____	____	____
	____	____	____	____
	____	____	____	____
	____	____	____	____
Unemployment taxes	____	____	____	____
	____	____	____	____
	____	____	____	____
	____	____	____	____
State Taxes				
Unemployment taxes	____	____	____	____
	____	____	____	____
	____	____	____	____
	____	____	____	____
Income taxes	____	____	____	____
Sales taxes	____	____	____	____
	____	____	____	____
	____	____	____	____
	____	____	____	____
Franchise taxes	____	____	____	____
Other	____	____	____	____
	____	____	____	____
	____	____	____	____
Local Taxes				
Sales taxes	____	____	____	____
	____	____	____	____
	____	____	____	____
	____	____	____	____
Real estate taxes	____	____	____	____
Personal property taxes	____	____	____	____
Licenses (retail, vending machine, etc.)	____	____	____	____
Other	____	____	____	____
	____	____	____	____
	____	____	____	____

to matching your employees' contributions to Social Security, however, use Form 940.) A return for each quarter is due on the last day of the following month—April 30, July 31, October 31, and January 31. In many cases remittance of these taxes is required before the return date is due; these dates depend on your situation. To make deposits you complete Form 501, Federal Tax Deposits, Withheld Income and FICA Taxes. This form, with a check, is sent to the Federal Reserve Bank that serves your district or a commercial bank that is authorized to accept such tax deposits. Your local bank or Federal Reserve Bank can give you the names of such commercial banks. In general, the smaller the amount of your tax liability, the less frequently you are required to make a deposit. The third step, matching the contribution, is done on Form 940. Any additional details are available from your local IRS office.

Excise Taxes

Federal excise taxes are due on the sale or use of certain items or certain transactions and on certain occupations. Normally a consultant is not involved in excise tax. However, to be absolutely certain, again check with your local IRS office.

Unemployment Taxes

If you paid wages of $1,500 or more in any calendar quarter, or you had one or more employees on at least some portion of one day in each of 20 or more calendar weeks, either consecutive or nonconsecutive, your consulting practice is liable for federal unemployment taxes. If this liability exceeds $200 for any calendar quarter and any preceding quarter, you must deposit the taxes in authorized commercial banks or a Federal Reserve Bank within one month following the close of the quarter. Each deposit must be accompanied by a preinscribed Form 508, Federal Unemployment Tax Deposit. A supply of these forms will be furnished to you automatically once you have applied for an employer identification number, which I will talk about shortly. But in any case, they may be obtained from the IRS where you file returns.

An annual return must be filed (on Form 940) on or before January 31 following the close of the calendar year for which the tax is due. Any tax still due is payable with the return. You must file Form 940 on a calendar-year basis even if you operate on a fiscal-year basis. You may wait until February 10 to file the form if the required deposits have been made on time and if you do not owe any additional tax. Usually the IRS will mail copies of Form 940 to you. But if not, be sure you obtain them from your local IRS office.

Obtaining an Employer Identification Number

This number is required for all employment tax returns to the federal government. You obtain this number by filing a Form SS–4 with your regional Internal Revenue Service Center. At the same time, you can ask for your business tax kit, IRS 454; it has additional information on taxes pertinent to each particular business or consulting practice with which you may be involved.

State and Local Taxes

State and local taxes vary by area. Three major types of state taxes are unemployment taxes, income taxes, and sales taxes, all of which have been discussed earlier. Every state has unemployment taxes; the rules vary by state and may not be the same as those of the federal government. Local taxes from counties, towns, and cities may include real estate, personal property taxes, taxes on receipt of businesses, and so forth. For more information on all these types of taxes, contact your local and state governments.

Minimizing Tax Paperwork

As you can see, many of the required taxes have to do with the fact that you have employees. If you do not have employees, the amount of paperwork is significantly reduced. Instead of hiring permanent staff for your company, try to retain individuals and pay them as consultants. There are some restrictions on how many hours or days someone may work for you and still be considered a consultant, so be sure to check on the current regulations if you do this.

For remitting all types of taxes, be certain to consult a good tax accountant. You will pay for the service, but this expert will save you far more in the long run.

EPILOGUE

There is no question in my mind that you can become a successful consultant (either full- or part-time) and make a valuable contribution to your client and to society at the same time. Everything you need to know in order to market and put into practice your own expertise in any particular field has already been given to you in the pages of this book. The questions that remain unanswered are those that you will learn as you begin actual work as a consultant. This is as it should be, for certain aspects of your consulting work are unique not only to your category of consulting, type of industry, or geographical area but, more important, to your personality and way of doing business. All totaled, the answers to these questions constitute your differential advantage over all the others doing identical work, and a sustained differential advantage over your competition will be the primary factor in your success.

A great adventure awaits you with many challenges, some disappointments, and the thrill of victory along the way. Further, your journey will involve not only monetary rewards but also the satisfaction of doing what you want and doing it well.

But no book, regardless of how complete or thorough it may be, can begin this journey for you. This you must do for yourself. Without your beginning, your action, your taking the steps toward starting your consultancy, there can be nothing. Therefore, the rest is up to you. I wish you the great success that only you yourself can achieve.

APPENDIX A:
LIST OF REFERENCES USEFUL TO CONSULTANTS

General

Albert, Kenneth J. *How to Be Your Own Management Consultant*. New York: McGraw-Hill, 1978.
Fuchs, Jerome H. *Management Consultants in Action*. New York: Hawthorne Books, 1975.
———. *Making the Most of Management Consulting Services*. New York: AMACOM, 1975.
Greiner, Larry E., and Robert O. Metzger. *Consulting to Management*. Englewood Cliffs, NJ: Prentice-Hall, 1983.
Holtz, Herman. *How to Succeed as an Independent Consultant*. New York: John Wiley & Sons, Inc., 1983.
Hunt, Alfred. *The Management Consultant*. New York: John Wiley & Sons, Inc., 1977.
Kelley, Robert E. *Consulting*. New York: Charles Scribner's Sons, 1981.
Klein, Howard M. *Other People's Business—A Primer on Management Consultants*. New York: Mason/Charter, 1977.
The Consultant's Library—A collection of books for consultants published by Bermont Books, P.O. Box 309, Glenelg, MD 21737.

Consulting for the Government

Cohen, William A. *How to Sell to the Government*. New York: John Wiley & Sons, Inc., 1981.
Holtz, Herman. *The $100 Billion Market: How to Do Business with the U.S. Government*. New York: AMACOM, 1980.

Marketing for Small Business and Consultants

Cohen, William A., and Marshall E. Reddick. *Successful Marketing for Small Business*. New York: AMACOM, 1981.
———. *Direct Response Marketing*. New York: John Wiley & Sons, Inc., 1983.
Wilson, Aubrey. *The Marketing of Professional Services*. Maidenhead, UK: McGraw-Hill, 1972.

Problem-Solving for Consultants

Albert, Kenneth J., ed. *Handbook of Business Problem Solving*. New York: McGraw-Hill, 1980.

Chase, Cochrane, and Kenneth L. Barasch. *Marketing Problem Solver*, 2nd ed. Radnor, PA: Chilton Book Co., 1977.

Cohen, William A. *The Entrepreneur and Small Business Problem Solver*. New York: John Wiley & Sons, Inc., 1983.

Executive Search/Executive Job Finding

Boll, Carl R. *Executive Jobs Unlimited: Updated Edition*. New York: Macmillan, 1980.

Cohen, William A. *The Executive's Guide to Finding a Superior Job*, rev. ed. New York: AMACOM, 1983.

Conarroe, Richard R. *Executive Search*. New York: Van Nostrand Reinhold, 1976.

Cox, Allan J. *Confessions of a Corporate Headhunter*. New York: Trident Press, 1973.

Djeddah, Eli. *Moving Up*. Berkeley, CA: Ten Speed Press, 1978.

Wareham, John. *Secrets of a Corporate Headhunter*. New York: Atheneum, 1980.

Newsletters

Consultants News, Templeton Road, Fitzwilliam, NH 03447.

Consulting Opportunities Journal, 1629 K Street, NW, Suite 520, Washington, DC 20006.

APPENDIX B:
SAMPLE CONSULTANT'S BROCHURE

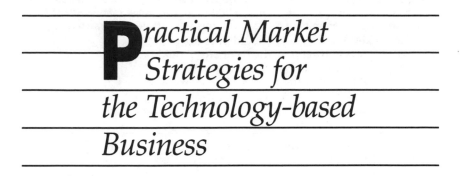

Practical Market
Strategies for
the Technology-based
Business

ROSENAU CONSULTING COMPANY

The Company

Rosenau Consulting Company was founded in 1978 to assist clients with marketing, new product development, and other aspects of technology management. Simply stated, we can assist management to define the main elements of a profitable business strategy, by analyzing:

- What markets the company should pursue;
- What products and services the company should provide;
- Why, how, and to what extent customers will buy;
- How to best introduce the new product or service.

What We Do

While the uniqueness of each client dictates the exact services needed, typically our services might include:

- Identification of market needs;
- Determination of market size and structure;
- Analysis of the competition;
- Delineation of product and service attributes which differentiate them from the competition;
- Market research and sales forecasting;
- Venture analysis and business planning;
- Evaluation and forecasting of changing technology;
- Technical audits;
- Facilitation of the development and introduction of the new product or service.

Clients

We have been involved with a wide variety of technologies and industries, but most of our clients manufacture or provide technology-based products or services for industrial and commercial markets. These have included:

- Corporations in the Fortune 500 list;
- Foreign corporations;
- Smaller companies;
- Service businesses;
- Individual investors and entrepreneurs.

Qualifications

Milton D. Rosenau, Jr., is a Certified Management Consultant (CMC). Before founding Rosenau Consulting Company in 1978, he was Vice President for Science and Technology at Avery International. Preceding that he had been Vice President and General Manager at Optigon Research and Development Corporation, now, a division of Vivitar. And for seventeen years before that he worked for The Perkin-Elmer Corporation in management, marketing and engineering.

His major accomplishments in these industrial positions include successful commercial product diversification from technology developed on government contract programs as well as new product development for consumer and industrial markets.

He recently authored *Innovation: Managing the Development of Profitable New Products* which has been variously reviewed as "excellent reading for both entrepreneurs and managers" and "an outstanding practical guide...for developing the new product from the original idea through the stages of strategic planning, business organization, production, and marketing the finished product." His previous book was *Successful Project Management*.

Mr. Rosenau's degree in Engineering Physics from Cornell University was followed by management programs at MIT, Cornell, and UCLA. He is a member of several professional groups, has lectured frequently, and has authored numerous articles in addition to the above mentioned books.

ROSENAU CONSULTING COMPANY

Recent Assignments

Marketing

- Corporate market and product strategy formulation
- Marketing and licensing direction for proprietary technology
- Market and technology analysis for corporate five-year plan
- Market planning for software mail-order business
- Market analysis of product concept to establish appropriate R&D program
- Advice on consumer product importation and distribution
- Survey of threats to and viability of new retail service concept

New Product Development

- Market studies: automated inspection of printed circuit boards, fiber optic transducers, and video display microscopes
- Critical path network for new product introduction
- New product strategy and idea brainstorming
- Technical and market analysis of photogrammetric instrument
- Radiation curing market study to identify unfilled requirements
- Development of market-based product qualification standard
- Appraisal of solar energy venture
- Systems and business analysis of lasers for a product application
- Review of major retroreflective product development program
- Guidance on establishing a procedure for new product development

Technology Management

- Recommendation on how to introduce project management capability
- Guidance on the proposed use of computers in a laboratory
- Specification of experiments to evaluate electron-beam curing process
- Assistance to research laboratory director to help increase productivity
- Attitude survey of R&D department personnel
- Training seminars

General

- Business strategy guidance
- Specification of position to be filled by an executive recruiter
- Counselling on career development options
- Time management assistance

ROSENAU CONSULTING COMPANY

O*ur Code of Professional Responsibility*

The basic responsibility of every *Certified Management Consultant* (CMC) is to put the interests of clients ahead of his or her own, and to serve them with integrity and competence.

As a CMC, Mr. Rosenau and his company agree to abide with all the professional ethics implied by that title.

We know that we are being hired for independent judgement and objectivity, technical expertise, analytical skill and concentrated attention to the solution of a problem. We will provide those skills. We will be impartial.

We will guard the confidentiality of all client information. We will not take financial gain or any other kind of advantage based on inside information. We will not serve two or more competing clients on sensitive problems without obtaining the approval of each client to do so. We will inform the client of any circumstances which might influence our judgement or objectivity.

Before accepting an assignment, we will confer with the client in sufficient detail to understand the problem and the scope of study needed to solve it. Such preliminary consultations are conducted confidentially, on terms agreed to by the client.

We will accept only those assignments we are qualified to perform which will provide real benefit to the client. But we cannot guarantee any specific results, such as the amount of cost reduction or profit increase. We present our qualifications on the basis of competence and experience. We perform each assignment on an individualized basis, and develop recommendations specifically for the practical solution of each client problem.

Whenever feasible, we agree with the client in advance on the fee basis for an assignment. We do not accept commissions or pay them to others for client referrals. Nor may we accept fees or commissions from others for recommending equipment, supplies, or services to his or her clients, as this would affect our impartiality.

ROSENAU CONSULTING COMPANY

Contractual Terms and Conditions

Professional time of M.D. Rosenau will be billed as either a fixed fee (if the required result can be precisely defined) or at an hourly rate quoted upon agreement of the scope of the effort.

In addition, the client will reimburse all expenses, plus a 20% handling charge added to these expenses. These expenses will be estimated upon agreement of the project's scope; if the actual expenses exceed the agreed estimate, the client will reimburse such excess expenses, but will not be charged any further handling charge on the additional amount.

Expenses include all out of pocket costs such as travel, telephone, printing and copying, postage, user fees for on-line information retrieval, publications, independent contractor assistance, and similar items. Other costs such as word processing, and mileage will be treated as expenses at rates approximating local commercial charges. Detailed expense records are maintained in our office and may be inspected if desired.

If travel costs are incurred on a trip that serves two or more clients, common travel costs will be allocated to each client in proportion to costs that would have been incurred for travel dedicated solely to each client alone.

Bills will be submitted twice a month, normally on the first and fifteenth. Bills are due and payable when submitted. A late payment charge of 1-1/2% per month (18% annually) may be applied to amounts outstanding ten (10) days after the date of the statement.

The client always has the right to terminate the assignment upon written notice. In such a case the client has no liability for charges beyond those incurred on their behalf through the date when notice of termination is received by us.

Because we cannot serve a client under terms or conditions that might impair our objectivity, independence, or integrity, Rosenau Consulting Company reserves the right to withdraw from the assignment if conditions develop to interfere with the successful completion of the assignment (except where our efforts are integral with the client's efforts).

It is understood that Rosenau Consulting Company and its contractors, if any, shall be in the relation of independent contractors with the client, and nothing herein shall be construed as designating us as employees or agents of the client for any purpose.

Rosenau Consulting Company will guard as confidential all information concerning the affairs of the client that is gathered during the course of the assignment. We agree to hold such information in strict confidence, and not to disclose it to others for a period of five years or until such information is otherwise released by the client.

Rosenau Consulting Company will not serve two or more competing clients in areas of vital interest without first informing each client.

The rights to any inventions that result from our work will be assigned to the client without any further charge for professional time. The client is responsible for all legal fees and similar expenses necessary to obtain patents that the client may desire to register.

ROSENAU CONSULTING COMPANY

Case History

Client Problem A small direct response advertiser sold microcomputer software by mail and wanted to grow. The industry was very competitive with sales volume obtained primarily by low discounted prices. They wanted to develop a strategic market plan which would permit them to outperform their industry competition.

What We Did Rosenau Consulting Company first examined their sales records and segmented their existing market. We obtained industry data to establish their market share and industry trend. We then interviewed industry experts, past customers, and a few prospective customers. This gave us enough information to help the client conduct economical mail surveys of customers and potential customers.

Result The client was able to selectively raise prices by providing other value to buyers. A new advertising and public relations campaign was initiated to convey this.

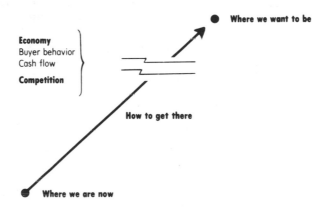

ROSENAU CONSULTING COMPANY

Case History

Client Problem A prior client received two recent inquiries about using one of their standard products or modifications of it to scan printed circuit boards. The purpose of the intended scanning was to rapidly and reliably locate defects on the printed circuit boards.

Because the client was not then serving that market, they retained us to estimate the market need and determine whether there was significant competition.

What We Did Rosenau Consulting Company quickly surveyed the available secondary market data using our on-line information retrieval system. We also conducted telephone interviews with potential users, industry experts, and providers of other test equipment. Simultaneously, we used an associate consultant to conduct field interviews.

Result In just a few months we were able to tell the client the approximate size of the market, to identify the nature of the competition, and, most importantly, to indicate the key product attributes that the design engineers would have to provide in a viable product. The client then initiated a joint venture development program.

ROSENAU CONSULTING COMPANY

How We Work

We cannot begin solving your specific problem until we first gain a solid basic understanding of it. In our initial contact we try to learn:

- Specific needs and background;
- Origins of the problem;
- Scope of the investigation;
- Key issues to be examined.

At this time we try to determine:

- A broad definition of the assignment and expected results;
- The information gathering methodology;
- Logical phases (if practical);
- Approximate time and cost.

At this initial point there is no obligation on either side. Once gathered, the above information helps the client decide whether we are the best people to handle the assignment, and helps us determine if we can do the job and whether we can do it properly in the time available.

When appropriate, the details and results of this discussion are confirmed in a written proposal outlining:

- Our understanding of the assignment;
- Suggested approach;
- Type and extent of client involvement;
- Organization of the work;
- Expected results;
- Estimated time and cost.

The client has no obligation until our proposal is accepted.

During each assignment, periodic updates are given. These are augmented by at least one interim review to summarize our findings to date and discuss any modifications in the direction for the balance of the project. Upon completion of our work, we report our findings and recommendations to client management, normally in the form of a briefing presentation. While structured, this presentation encourages the questioning and discussion of our findings. Our goal is to provide clients with recommendations which are practical for them to implement. The presentation is then documented with a written report.

Fees are based on the time needed plus expenses actually incurred in carrying out the assignment. More detail may be found on the "Contractual Terms and Conditions" insert.

Why Retain Rosenau Consulting Company?

1. Expertise We are not trying to be all things to all people. We offer a specialized service in management consulting concerning the development of profitable new products and services. We have great experience and expertise in our chosen specialization. Milton D. Rosenau, Jr., founder, has extensive functional and general management experience in this area. Associate consultants are also utilized when their experience is relevant and helpful to the client.

2. Efficiency Because we are specialized, we have files and tools that often allow us to perform an assignment better, faster, and cheaper than clients can on their own. We can interrogate on-line information data bases. This offers two benefits: It decreases the amount of time we need to spend in the field, and it makes our fieldwork yield better results because it is well focused.

3. Concentration Because we can concentrate on accomplishing a critical assignment quickly, our clients are freed to operate the on-going business without diversion.

4. Anonymity Because we are an independent firm, we need not reveal the identity or purpose of our clients, within normal legal and ethical bounds. And we will not reveal critical information without prior approval.

5. Objectivity We bring a fresh viewpoint, unencumbered by hierarchical pressure or bias. If we cannot help our client, we will say so and refer them to other appropriate sources. We will never be used simply as an outside stamp of approval on an executive's pet project.

Client Relationships

Work is carried out in a manner which best satisfies the client in accordance with the Code of Professional Practice of the Association of Management Consultants (of which Rosenau Consulting Company is a member). This can be arranged by either a retainer for a stipulated period or, more commonly, as a single project assignment. Milton D. Rosenau, Jr., CMC, directs all assignments and client relations. Specialist associate consultants are called upon as needed.

APPENDIX C:
THE CONSULTANT'S
QUESTIONNAIRE AND AUDIT

Company: _____

Division: _____

Address: _____

City, State, and Zip Code: _____

Other Division Locations: _____

_____

_____

_____

Company Officers and Other Key Executives: _____

_____

_____

_____

Primary Contact for This Engagement: _____

Title: _____

Address: _____

City, State, and Zip Code: _____

Phone Number: _____

Backup Contact for This Engagement: _____

Title: _____

Address: _____

City, State, and Zip Code: _____

Phone Number: _____

PART I—PRODUCTION

What % of production is:		What % of production is:	
Job-order (custom) manufacture	_____ %	Private label	_____ %
Repetitive (standard) manufacture	_____ %	Sold under your own name	_____ %
	100%		100%

Do you subcontract?   Yes _____   No _____
If yes, what % of your total work? _____%
Who are your major subcontractors? _____
_____
_____
_____
_____

Are you satisfied with their work?   Yes _____   No _____

What % of your production do you export? _____%
What countries do you export to? Which are your biggest customers? ___
_____
_____
_____
_____

At what current % of production capacity are you now operating? ___%.
What additional % could you add, to total capacity (100%), in order to
accommodate additional sales? _____%.
How many months would it take to reach this figure? _____months.
What is the minimum % of capacity at which you must operate in order
to break even? _____%.

How seasonal is your production?
not at all _____   slightly _____   fairly _____   highly_____   totally _____
At which season(s) is production at its peak? _____
At which season(s) is production at its minimum? _____

To what extent are your production operations regulated by federal, state,
or local government?
_____
_____
_____

Who are your major suppliers? Are you satisfied with them?
_____
_____
_____
_____

PART II—MARKETS SERVED

If accurate figures are unavailable,
give estimates to the following questions:

	Last year	3 years ago
Total industry sales	$____	$____
Your sales	$____	$____
Your market share	$____	$____
Major competition's share	____%	____%
2nd-ranking competitor's share	____%	____%
3rd-ranking competitor's share	____%	____%

Consumer Market ____%
Industrial Market ____%

Describe each consumer market or industrial market by SIC code. List your products, the channels used to distribute them, and your approximate % share of each market.

MARKET	PRODUCTS	CHANNEL(S)	MARKET SHARE

List your major competitors.

	Name	Strongest markets	Why strong in these markets?	Strongest products	Why strong with these products?
1. ____		_____	_____	_____	_____
Address: ____					
2. ____		_____	_____	_____	_____
Address: ____					
3. ____		_____	_____	_____	_____
Address: ____					

What new competitors have entered the marketplace in the past three years?

_____

Have any done unusually well? If so, in what markets, with what products, and why?

_____

_____

_____

PART III—PRODUCTS

Approximately how many different individual products do you manufacture? _____

What is the size in dollars of your average sale (to your end-customer)?

_____

How many times is your average product purchased by the same customer in a single year?

_____

Approximately what % of your customers purchase from you again?

_____%.

What is the average purchase life of your customers? _____

Why do they stop buying from you? _____

Which of your products have the highest margins?

_____

_____

Do you sell any "loss leaders"? List them below:

_____

_____

Has their effectiveness ever been tested against that of other items? If so, which items, and how?

_____

_____

List your products below by sales and profits:

Product	Annual Sales	Annual Profits

_____
_____
_____

Have you considered dropping those products accounting for low profits? If low sales/profit products are being retained, indicate why.

_____
_____
_____
_____
_____
_____

Do you have an ongoing new product research and development program?

    Yes _____   No _____

When was your last new product introduced? _____

When was your last major product modification introduced? _____

How do you do new product research and development?

    in-house _____   subcontract _____

Why do you do new product research and development?

    meet the competition _____   new markets _____

    product obsolescence _____   increase sales _____

    reduce production   other _____

      costs   _____   _____

    reduce material costs _____

How do you screen potential products for development? _____

_____
_____

PART IV—MARKETING RESEARCH

Do you have an ongoing market research program? _____

Do you have correct information on:

Who's buying your products _____Why they're buying _____

Where your products are being bought _____Who's making the purchase decision _____ How to best reach your customers through advertising _____ The effectiveness of advertising programs _____ Your competitors' products _____ Your competitors' strategies _____

Potential markets _____ Relative effectiveness of different channels of distribution _____ New applications of your products _____ Export potential _____ Related products demanded by your customers _____

Relative effectiveness and efficiency of salespeople _____ Packaging
effectiveness _____ Pricing sensitivity _____ Image and positioning
of your product relative to others _____Publicity possibilities _____
Operating ratios in your industry _____
What trade associations do you belong to? _____
_____
_____

What trade magazines or journals do you subscribe to? _____
_____
_____
_____

Do you rely on the market research available from associations and magazines?
     Yes _____   No _____
If you make use of internally generated market research, which organizations within your company provide this research, and what research do
they provide? _____
_____
_____
_____

What outside organizations have assisted you in doing research? _____
_____
_____
_____

PART V—MARKET SEGMENTS

Consumer Market

What segments of the market are your present customers? _____
_____
_____
_____

Are your products more habitual purchase _____, impulse _____, or
planned purchase _____?
In your market, which are the most important factors for buying?
Price _____ Quality _____ Features _____ Performance _____
Appearance _____ Others _____
_____

Who influences the decision to buy your products?
Husbands _____Wives _____Children _____Doctors _____
Dentists _____Educators _____Beauticians _____Barbers _____

Lawyers _____Religious leaders _____Mechanics _____
Contractors _____Tradesmen _____Fraternal or social
groups _____High-income or influential people _____
Others _____

Industrial Market

Who makes the purchase decision for your product?

_____

_____

_____

Outline the sequence of events as to how this decision is made. Include
other factors or individuals influencing this decision.

_____

_____

_____

_____

_____

_____

PART VI—PRICING

How do you decide on the price for your products? _____

_____

_____

What's your warranty policy? _____

_____

_____

What's your service policy? _____

_____

_____

_____

Any other special policies of importance? _____

_____

_____

_____

Pricing Checklist*

Examining Costs, Sales Volume, and Profits

The questions in this part should be helpful when you look at prices from the viewpoint of costs, sales volume, and profits.

Costs and Prices

The company that sets the price for an item by applying a standard markup may be overlooking certain cost factors that are connected with that item. The following questions are designed to help you gather information that should be helpful when you are determining prices on specific types of items.

	Yes	No
1. Do you know which of your operating costs remain the same regardless of sales volume?	____	____
2. Do you know which of your operating costs decrease percentage-wise as your sales volume increases?	____	____
3. Have you ever figured out the breakeven point for your items selling at varying price levels?	____	____
4. Do you look behind high gross margin percentages? (For example, a product with a high gross margin may also be a slow turnover item with high handling costs. Thus, it may be less profitable than lower margin items that turn over fast.)	____	____
5. When you select items for price reductions, do you project the effects on profits? (For example, if a food marketer considers whether to run canned ham or rump steak on sale, an important cost factor is labor. Practically none is involved in featuring canned ham; however, a rump steak sale requires the skill of a meat-cutter and this labor cost might mean little or no profits.)	____	____

Pricing and Sales Volume

An effective pricing program should also consider sales volume. For example, high prices might limit your sales volume while low prices might result in a large but unprofitable volume. The following questions should be helpful in determining what is right for your situation.

*This section (which continues until the beginning of Part VII) is adapted from Joseph D. O'Brien, "A Pricing Checklist for Managers," Small Business Administration, 1972.

		Yes	No
6.	Have you considered setting a sales volume goal and then studying to see if your prices will help you reach it?	____	____
7.	Have you set a target of a certain number of new customers for next year? (If so, how can pricing help you to get them?) _____		

8. Should you limit the quantities of low-margin items that any one customer can buy when such items are on sale? (If so, will you advertise this policy?) _____

9. What is your policy when a sale item is sold out before the end of the advertised period? Do you allow disappointed customers to buy the item later at the sale price? _____

Pricing and Profits

Prices should help bring in sales that are profitable over the long pull. The following questions are designed to help you think about pricing policies and their effect on your annual profits.

		Yes	No
10.	Do you have all the facts on costs, sales, and competitive behavior?	____	____
11.	Do you set prices with the hope of accomplishing definite objectives, such as a 1% profit increase over last year?	____	____
12.	Have you set a given level of profits in dollars and in percent of sales?	____	____
13.	Do you keep records to give you the needed facts on profits, losses, and prices?	____	____
14.	Do you review your pricing practices periodically to make sure that they are helping to achieve your profit goals?	____	____

Judging the Buyer, Timing, and Competitors

The questions in this part are designed to help you check your practices for judging the buyer (your customer), your timing, and your competitors.

The Buyer and Pricing Strategy

After you have your facts on costs, the next point must be the *customer*—whether you are changing a price, putting in a new item, or checking out your present price practices. Knowledge of your customers helps you determine how to vary prices in order to get the average gross margin you need for making a profit. (For example, to get an average gross margin of 35%, some retailers put a low markup—10%, for instance—on items that they promote as traffic builders and use high markup—sometimes as much as 60%—on slow-moving items.) The following questions should be helpful in checking your knowledge about your customers.

	Yes	No
15. Do you know whether your customers shop around and for what items?	____	____
16. Do you know how your customers make their comparisons? By reading newspaper ads? Store shopping? Hearsay? _____		
17. Are you trying to appeal to customers who buy on price alone? To those who buy on quality alone? To those who combine the two? _____		
18. Do any of your customers tell you that your prices are in line with those of your competitors? Higher? Lower? _____		
19. Do you know which item (or types of items) your customers call for even though you raise the price?	____	____
20. Do you know which item (or types of items) your customers leave on your shelves when you raise the price?	____	____
21. Do certain items seem to appeal to customers more than others when you run weekend, clearance, or special-day sales?	____	____
22. Have you used your individual sales records to classify your present customers according to the volume of their purchases?	____	____
23. Will your customers buy more if you use multiple pricing (for example, 3 for 39 cents for products with rapid turnover)?	____	____
24. Do your customers respond to odd prices more readily than to even prices, for example, 99 cents rather than $1?	____	____

25. Have you decided on a pricing strategy to create a favorable price image with your customers? (For example, a retailer with 8,000 different items might decide to make a full margin on all medium or slow movers while featuring—at low price levels—the remaining fast movers.) ____ ____

26. If you are trying to build a quality price image, do your individual customer records, such as charge account statements, show that you are selling a larger number of higher priced items than you were 12 months ago? ____ ____

27. Do your records of individual customer accounts and your observations of customer behavior in the store show price as the important factor in their buying? Service? Assortments? Some other consideration? _____

Time and Pricing

Effective merchandising means that you have the right product, at the right place, at the right price, and at the right time. All are important, but timing is the critical element for the smaller retailer. The following questions should be helpful in determining what is the right time for you to adjust prices.

	Yes	No

28. Are you a "leader" (rather than a "follower") in announcing your price reductions? (Followers, even though they match their competitors, create a negative impression on their customers.) ____ ____

29. Have you studied your competitors to see whether they follow any sort of pattern when making price changes? (For example, do some of them run clearance sales earlier than others?) ____ ____

30. Is there a pattern to the kinds of items that competitors promote at lower prices at certain times of the month or year? ____ ____

31. Have you decided whether it is better to take early mark-downs on seasonal or style goods or to run a clearance sale at the end of the season? ____ ____

32. Have you made regular annual sales, such as Anniversary Sales, Fall Clearance, or Holiday Cleanup,

so popular that many customers wait for them
rather than buying in season?   _____   _____

33. When you change a price, do you make sure that
     all customers know about it through price tags and
     so on?   _____   _____

34. Do you try to time price reductions so they can be
     promoted in your advertising?   _____   _____

Competition and Pricing

When you set prices, you have to consider how your competitors might
react to your prices. The starting place is learning as much as you can
about their price structures. The following questions are designed to help
you check out this phase of pricing.

                                                                  Yes   No

35. Do you use all the available channels of information
     to keep you up-to-date on your competitors' price
     policies? (Some useful sources of information are:
     things your customers tell you; competitors' price
     lists and catalogs, if used; competitors' advertising;
     reports from your suppliers; trade paper studies;
     and shoppers employed by you.)   _____   _____

36. Should your policy be to always try to sell above or
     below competition? Or only to meet the competi-
     tion? _____

     _____

37. Is there a pattern to the way your competitors re-
     spond to your price cuts?   _____   _____

38. Is the leader pricing of your competitors affecting
     your sales volume to such an extent that you must
     alter your pricing policy on individual items (or
     types of items) of merchandise?   _____   _____

39. Do you realize that no two competitors have iden-
     tical cost curves? (This difference in costs means
     that certain price levels may be profitable for you
     but unprofitable for your competitor or vice versa.)   _____   _____

Practices That Can Help Offset Price

Some companies take advantage of the fact that price is not always the
determining factor in making a sale. They supply customer services and
offer other inducements to offset the effect of competitors' lower prices.

Delivery service is an example. Providing a comfortable shoppers' meeting place is another. The following questions are designed to help you take a look at some of these practices.

		Yes	No
40.	Do the items or services you sell have advantages for which customers are willing to pay a little more?	____	____
41.	From personal observation of customer behavior in your store, can you tell about how much more customers will pay for such advantages?	____	____
42.	Should you change your services so as to create an advantage for which your customers will be willing to pay?	____	____
43.	Does your advertising emphasize customer benefits rather than price?	____	____
44.	Are you using the most common nonprice competitive tools? (For example, have you tried to alter your product or service to the existing market? Have you tried stamps, bonus purchase gifts, or other plans for building repeat business?)	____	____
45.	Should policies on returned goods be changed so as to better impress your customers?	____	____
46.	If you sell repair services, have you checked out your guarantee policy?	____	____
47.	Should you alter assortments of merchandise to increase sales?	____	____

PART VII—SALES AND DISTRIBUTION

How much of your product line is:

Manufactured by you   ____%
Manufactured for you
   by someone else   ____%
                                        100%

Is your distribution:
Regional _____   National _____   International _____
If regional, in what areas? _____

_____

If national, what are your strongest areas? _____

_____

If international, what are your strongest foreign countries? _____
_____
_____

What systems of distribution do you use?
_____
_____
_____
_____

How do you subdivide your product lines in your sales organization?
Geographical territories ___   Type of customer ___   Type of product ___
Other _____

Do your salespeople, agents, or distributors have exclusive territories?
_____
_____
_____

How many people do you have selling your product, and what are their
responsibilities?
_____
_____
_____

How do you compensate your salespeople?
_____
_____

Do you offer any special sales incentives?
_____
_____

Who prepares your product catalogs?
_____
_____
_____

What aids to selling do you *or your distributor or agent* provide to people
selling your product?
_____
_____
_____
_____

Do you provide any type of formal sales training? Explain type, subjects, length of programs, etc.

_____

_____

_____

_____

How frequently do you hold sales meetings or conferences? What subjects are covered?

_____

_____

_____

What branch offices do you maintain?

_____

_____

_____

How do you select your agents and distributors?

_____

_____

_____

_____

How do you set sales quotas?

_____

_____

_____

What trade discounts do you offer?

_____

_____

_____

What terms of sale do you use?

_____

_____

Do you grant any special concessions or offers to stimulate sales?

_____

_____

What is your % of returned goods? _____%

What is your % of goods returned due to damage? _____%
What is your % of bad debts? _____%
What is the average time for collection of amounts owed to you? _____
How frequently do your salespeople send in reports? _____
How do you maintain your sales records?

_____
_____
_____

What is your ratio of sales made to number of calls made?

_____

Are your "cold calls" supplemented by any other type of communication
such as direct mail? _____

_____
_____
_____

How do you control your salespeople's activities?

_____
_____
_____
_____

What % of your salespeople's time is spent on

planning	_____%
preparation	_____%
travel	_____%
calls on prospects	_____%
calls on established customers	_____%
other	_____%
	100%

What are the following yearly gross sales figures of your salespeople?

average gross	$ _____
lowest gross	$ _____
highest gross	$ _____

What is the average amount spent on promotion activities that back up
sales per salesperson per year?

   (Total spent yearly on sales promotion, advertising, publicity divided by number of salespeople) $ _____

What is the average amount spent on sales activities per saleperson per
year?

   (Total spent on recruiting, training, expense accounts, and compensation divided by number of salespeople) $ _____

What are your best wholesale outlets? _____

_____

_____

What are your worst wholesale outlets? _____

_____

_____

What merchandising techniques are used by your best outlets?

_____

_____

What are your best retail outlets?

_____

_____

_____

What are your worst retail outlets?

_____

_____

_____

What merchandising techniques are used by your best retail outlets?

_____

_____

_____

What merchandising help do you make available to these outlets? Which is being used successfully? Unsuccessfully?

_____

_____

_____

PART VIII—ADVERTISING

What media do you use to promote to your customers?

_____

_____

_____

What advertising have you done, and what were the costs over the last year? What were the results?

_____
_____
_____
_____
_____
_____
_____

How were results measured for these ads?

_____
_____
_____
_____

Do you have an advertising agency?   Yes _____   No _____

    If yes,   Name _____
                Contact _____
                Address _____
                Phone No. _____

PART IX—PUBLICITY AND PUBLIC RELATIONS

What type of public relations program did you engage in over the previous year? What were the costs, and what were the results?

_____
_____
_____
_____
_____
_____
_____
_____
_____

PART X—MANAGEMENT OPERATIONS

What type of planning does the organization do?

_____
_____
_____

How is budgetary control of operations maintained?

PART XI—FINANCIAL CHECKLIST*

Are You Making a Profit?

Analysis of Revenues and Expenses. Since profit is revenues less expenses, to determine what your profit is you must first identify all revenues and expenses for the period under study.

	Yes	No
1. Have you chosen an appropriate period for profit determination?	___	___

For accounting purposes firms generally use a 12-month period, such as January 1 to December 31 or July 1 to June 30. The accounting year you select doesn't have to be a calendar year (January to December); a seasonal business, for example, might close its year after the end of the season. The selection depends upon the nature of your business, your personal preference, or possible tax considerations.

2. Have you determined your total revenues for the accounting period?   ___   ___

In order to answer this question, consider the following questions:

What is the amount of gross revenue from sales of your goods or service? (*Gross Sales*)

What is the amount of goods returned by your customers and credited? (*Returns and Rejects*)

What is the amount of discounts given to your customers and employees? (*Discounts*)

What is the amount of net sales from goods and services? (*Net Sales = Gross Sales − [Returns and Rejects + Discounts]*)

*This section (which continues until the beginning of Part XII) is adapted from Narendra C. Bhandari and Charles S. McCubbin, Jr., "Checklist for Profit Watching," Small Business Administration, 1980.

What is the amount of income from other sources, such as interest on bank deposits, dividends from securities, and rent on property leased to others? (*Nonoperating Income*)

What is the amount of total revenue? (*Total Revenue = Net Sales + Nonoperating Income*)

3. Do you know what your total expenses are? _____ _____

Expenses are the cost of goods sold and services used in the process of selling goods or services. Some common expenses for all businesses are:

Cost of goods sold (Cost of Goods Sold = Beginning Inventory + Purchases − Ending Inventory)

Wages and salaries (Don't forget to include your own—at the actual rate you'd have to pay someone else to do your job.)

Rent

Utilities (electricity, gas, telephone, water, etc.)

Supplies (office, cleaning, and the like)

Delivery expenses

Insurance

Advertising and promotional costs

Maintenance and upkeep

Depreciation (Here you need to make sure your depreciation policies are realistic and that all depreciable items are included.)

Taxes and licenses

Interest

Bad debts

Professional assistance (accountant, attorney, etc.)

There are, of course, many other types of expenses, but the point is that every expense must be recorded and deducted from your revenues before you know what your profit is. Understanding your expenses is the first step toward *controlling them* and *increasing your profit*.

Financial Ratios

A *financial ratio* is an expression of the relationship between two items selected from the income statement or the balance sheet. Ratio analysis helps you evaluate the weak and strong points in your financial and managerial performance.

4. Do you know your *current ratio*?

The *current ratio* (current assets divided by current debts) is a measure of the cash or near cash position (liquidity) of the firm. It tells you if you have enough cash to pay your firm's current creditors. The higher the ratio, the more liquid the firm's position is and, hence, the higher the credibility of the firm. Cash, receivables, marketable securities, and inventory are current assets. Naturally, you need to be realistic in valuing receivables and inventory for a true picture of your liquidity, since some debts may be uncollectable and some stock obsolete. Current liabilities are those that must be paid in one year.

5. Do you know your *quick ratio*?

Quick assets are current assets minus inventory. The *quick ratio* (or acid-test ratio) is found by dividing quick assets by current liabilities. The purpose, again, is to test the firm's ability to meet its current obligations. This test doesn't include inventory to make it a stiffer test of the company's liquidity. It tells you if the business could meet its current obligations with quickly convertible assets should sales revenues suddenly cease.

6. Do you know your total debt to net worth ratio?

This ratio (the result of total debt divided by net worth, then multiplied by 100) is a measure of how the company can meet its total obligations from equity. The lower the ratio, the higher the proportion of equity relative to debt and the better the firm's credit rating will be.

7. Do you know your average collection period?

You find this ratio by dividing accounts receivable by daily credit sales. (Daily credit sales = annual credit sales divided by 360.) This ratio tells you the length of time it takes the firm to get its cash after making a sale on credit. The shorter this period, the quicker the cash inflow is. A longer than normal period may mean overdue and uncollectable bills. If you extend credit for a specific period (say, 30 days), this ratio should be very close to the same number of days. If it's much longer than the established period, you may need to alter your credit policies. It's wise to develop an aging schedule to gauge the trend of collections and identify slow payers. Slow collections (without adequate financing charges) hurt your profit, since you could be doing something much more useful with your money, such as taking advantage of discounts on your own payables.

8. Do you know your ratio of net sales to total assets?

This ratio (net sales divided by total assets) measures the efficiency with which you are using your assets. A higher than normal ratio indicates that the firm is able to generate sales from its assets faster (and better) than the average concern.

9. Do you know your operating profit to net sales ratio?

This ratio (the result of dividing operating profit by net sales and multiplying by 100) is most often used to determine the profit position relative to sales. A higher than normal ratio indicates that your sales are good, that your expenses are low, or both. Interest income and interest expense should not be included in calculating this ratio.

10. Do you know your net profit to total assets ratio?

This ratio (found by multiplying by 100 the result of dividing net profit by total assets) is often called return on investment or ROI. It focuses on the profitability of the overall operation of the firm. Thus, it allows management to measure the effects of its policies on the firm's profitability. The ROI is the single most important measure of a firm's financial position. You might say it's the bottom line for the bottom line.

11. Do you know your net profit to net worth ratio?

This ratio is found by dividing net profit by net worth and multiplying the result by 100. It provides information on the productivity of the resources the owners have committed to the firm's operations.

All ratios measuring profitability can be computed either before or after taxes, depending on the purpose of the computations. Ratios have limitations. Since the information used to derive ratios is itself based on accounting rules and personal judgments, as well as facts, the ratios cannot be considered absolute indicators of a firm's financial position. Ratios are only one means of assessing the performance of the firm and must be considered in perspective with many other measures. They should be used as a point of departure for further analysis and not as an end in themselves.

Sufficiency of Profit

The following questions are designed to help you measure the adequacy of the profit your firm is making. Making a profit is only the first step; making enough profit to survive and *grow* is really what business is all about.

	Yes	No
12. Have you compared your profit with your profit goals?	____	____
13. Is it possible your goals are too high or too low?	____	____
14. Have you compared your present profits (absolute and ratios) with the profits made in the last one to three years?	____	____
15. Have you compared your profits (absolute and ratios) with profits made by similar firms in your line?	____	____

A number of organizations publish financial ratios for various businesses, among them Dun & Bradstreet, Robert Morris Associates, the Accounting Corporation of America, NCR Corporation, and the Bank of America. Your own trade association may also publish such studies. Remember, these published ratios are only averages. You probably want to be better than average.

Trend of Profit

	Yes	No
16. Have you analyzed the direction your profits have been taking?	____	____

The preceding analyses, with all their merits, report on a firm only at a single time in the past. It is not possible to use these isolated moments to indicate the trend of your firm's performance. To do a trend analysis, performance indicators (absolute amounts or ratios) should be computed for several time periods (yearly for several years, for example) and the results laid out in columns side by side for easy comparison. You can then evaluate your performance, see the direction it's taking, and make initial forecasts of where it will go.

Mix of Profit

Yes   No

17. Does your firm sell more than one major product line or provide several distinct services?   _____ _____

If it does, a separate profit and ratio analysis of each should be made: to show the relative contribution by each product line or service; to show the relative burden of expenses by each product or service; to show which items are most profitable, which are less so, and which are losing money; and to show which are slow and fast moving.

The profit and ratio analyses of each major item help you find out the strong and weak areas of your operations. They can help you to make profit-increasing decisions to drop a product line or service or to place particular emphasis behind one or another.

Records

Good records are essential. Without them a firm doesn't know where it's been, where it is, or where it's heading. Keeping records that are accurate, up-to-date, and easy to use is one of the most important functions of the owner-manager, his or her staff, and his or her outside counselors (lawyer, accountant, banker).

Basic Records

Yes   No

18. Do you have a general journal and/or special journals, such as one for cash receipts and disbursements?   _____ _____

A general journal is the basic record of the firm. Every monetary event in the life of the firm is entered in the general journal or in one of the special journals.

19. Do you prepare a sales report or analysis?   _____ _____

    (a) Do you have sales goals by product, department, and accounting period (month, quarter, year)?   _____ _____

(b) Are your goals reasonable?   ____ ____

(c) Are you meeting your goals?   ____ ____

If you aren't meeting your goals, try to list the likely reasons on a sheet of paper. Such a study might include areas such as general business climate, competition, pricing, advertising, sales promotion, credit policies, and the like. Once you've identified the apparent causes you can take steps to increase sales (and profits).

Buying and Inventory System

	Yes	No

20. Do you have a buying and inventory system?   ____ ____

The buying and inventory systems are two critical areas of a firm's operation that can affect profitability.

21. Do you keep records on the quality, service, price, and promptness of delivery of your sources of supply?

22. Have you analyzed the advantages and disadvantages of:

(a) Buying from suppliers?   ____ ____

(b) Buying from a minimum number of suppliers?   ____ ____

23. Have you analyzed the advantages and disadvantages of buying through cooperatives or other such systems?   ____ ____

24. Do you know:

(a) How long it usually takes to receive each order?   ____ ____

(b) How much inventory cushion (usually called safety stock) to have so you can maintain normal sales while you wait for the order to arrive?   ____ ____

25. Have you ever suffered because you were out of stock?   ____ ____

26. Do you know the optimum order quantity for each item you need?   ____ ____

27. Do you (or can you) take advantage of quantity discounts for large-size single purchases?   ____ ____

28. Do you know your costs of ordering inventory and carrying inventory?   ____ ____

The more frequently you buy (smaller quantities per order), the higher your average ordering costs (clerical costs, postage, telephone costs, etc.) will be, and the lower the average carrying costs (storage, loss through pilferage, obsolescence, etc.) will be. On the other hand, the larger the quantity per order, the lower the average ordering cost and the higher the carrying costs. A balance should be struck so that the minimum cost overall for ordering and carrying inventory can be achieved.

29. Do you keep records of inventory for each item?

These records should be kept current by making entries whenever items are added to or removed from inventory. Simple records on $3'' \times 5''$ or $5'' \times 7''$ cards can be used with each item being listed on a separate card. Proper records will show for each item: quantity in stock, quantity on order, date of order, slow or fast seller, and valuations (which are important for taxes and your own analyses).

Other Financial Records

Yes   No

30. Do you have an accounts payable ledger?

This ledger will show what, whom, and why you owe. Such records should help you make your payments on schedule. Any expense not paid on time could adversely affect your credit, but even more importantly, such records should help you take advantage of discounts that can help boost your profits.

31. Do you have an accounts receivable ledger?

This ledger will show who owes money to your firm. It will show how much is owed, how long it has been outstanding, and why the money is owed. Overdue accounts could indicate that your credit granting policy needs to be reviewed and that you may not be getting the cash into the firm quickly enough to pay your own bills at the optimum time.

32. Do you have a cash receipts journal?

This journal records the cash received by source, day, and amount.

33. Do you have a cash payments journal?

This journal will be similar to the cash receipts journal but will show cash paid out instead of cash received. The two cash journals can be combined, if convenient.

34. Do you prepare an income (profit and loss or P&L) statement and a balance sheet?   ____   ____

These are statements about the condition of your firm at a specific time and show the income, expenses, assets, and liabilities of the firm. They are absolutely essential.

35. Do you prepare a budget?   ____   ____

You could think of a budget as a "record in advance," projecting "future" inflows and outflows for your business. A budget is usually prepared for a single year, generally to correspond with the accounting year. It is then, however, broken down into quarterly and monthly projections.

There are different kinds of budgets: cash, production, sales, etc. A cash budget, for example, will show the estimate of sales and expenses for a particular period of time. The cash budget forces the firm to think ahead by estimating its income and expenses. Once reasonable projections are made for every important product line or department, the owner-manager has set targets for employees to meet for sales and expenses. You must plan to assure a profit. And you must prepare a budget to plan.

PART XII—MATERIAL TO ASK FOR

Sales Brochures

Price Lists

Public Relations Materials

Product Description and Photographs

Special Forms

Annual Report

Financial Statements

Sample Advertisements and Promotional Materials

Information Given Out at Recent Trade Shows

APPENDIX D:
AN EXTENSIVE CONSULTING PROPOSAL

A PROPOSAL FOR A
PROJECT PLANNING AND CONTROL SYSTEM
PROCEDURE DEVELOPMENT PROGRAM

SUBMITTED TO:

XXXXXXXXXXXXXXXXXXXXXXXXXXXX
XXXXXXXXXXXXXXXXXXXXXXXXXXXX
XXXXXXXXXXXXXXXXXXXXXXXXXXXX

ATTENTION: XXXXXXXXXXXXXXXXXXXXX
XXXXXXXXXXXXXXXXXXXX

SUBMITTED BY:

DECISION PLANNING CORPORATION
3184-A AIRWAY AVENUE
COSTA MESA, CALIFORNIA 92626

All pages of this document contain information proprietary to Decision Planning Corporation. All data furnished in connection with this proposal shall not be duplicated, transmitted, used, or otherwise disclosed to anyone other than XXXXXXXXXXXXXXXXXXXXXXXXXXXXXXX, and then only for the purpose of evaluating the quotation. This restriction is applicable to all sheets of this proposal.

OCTOBER 15, 1985

TABLE OF CONTENTS

1.0   EXECUTIVE SUMMARY

Decision Planning Corporation (DPC) submits this proposal to XXXX-XXXXXXXXXXXX XXXXXXXXXXXXXXXXXXXXXXXXXX to develop Project Planning and Control System Procedures. The proposal contains a description of proposed services, associated schedule and costs, and DPC qualifications to assist XXXXXXXXXXXXXX in this program.

In order to facilitate evaluation of the subject matter, DPC has subdivided the proposal into four sections and two appendices. Following is a brief description of each part.

EXECUTIVE SUMMARY	The Executive Summary section provides an overview of the proposed program and the proposed approach to accomplishing contract work. The section concludes with a description of DPC qualifications to perform the proposed tasks.
TECHNICAL PROPOSAL	The Technical Proposal section begins with a detailed description of work to be accomplished and products/services to be delivered to XXXXXXXXXXXXXXXXXX XXXXXXXXX XXXXXXXXXXX. In addition to defining program scope, Section 2.0 identifies responsibilities of XXXXXXXXXXXXXXXXXXXXXXX XXXXXXXXXXXXX and Decision Planning Corporation for development, review, and approval of individual products and services.
COST PROPOSAL	The Cost Proposal section contains a detailed estimate of labor hours and other elements of cost necessary to accomplish the proposed scope. This section also presents assumptions upon which the proposal is based, labor rates, terms and conditions, and other information necessary to fully understand the Cost Proposal.
MANAGEMENT PROPOSAL	The Management Proposal section begins with a discussion of the approach and methodology that will be used in accomplishing the statement of work. A summary schedule of events is also shown. The section closes with a detailed examination of DPC's project

1

organization, both in terms of personnel to be assigned and the organization of personnel into the Project Team.

DPC concludes the proposal by providing two appendices containing data that describe DPC's overall qualifications and performance record. These appendices are presented outside the body of the proposal in order to maintain proposal continuity and thus facilitate its review. The subject appendices are described below.

Appendix A - DPC believes that its experience and knowledge in providing services offered in this proposal are the foremost in the industry. Appendix A, "Relevant DPC Experience," provides a synopsis of representative DPC accomplishments.

Appendix B - DPC is convinced that the qualifications and experience of the staff proposed for this program cannot be excelled by any of its competitors. Appendix B, "DPC Staff Resumes," depicts career accomplishments and the academic record of the DPC Program Team.

[Appendix A and Appendix B have been intentionally deleted.]

1.1 Program Background

XXXXXXXXXXXXXXX has initiated a corporate-wide effort to upgrade existing management information system hardware and software systems. In parallel with this effort, the Engineering Department has initiated an effort to upgrade its project planning and control system by revising existing procedures and/or developing new procedures which describe how

XXXXXXXXXXXXXXX organizes, plans, monitors, and controls project work on their engineering and construction projects.

Decision Planning Corporation recognizes the desire of XXXXX-XXXXXXXXXX to have these procedures defined, written, and implemented as soon as possible. The development of these types of procedures is normally accomplished in three distinct steps. The first step involves defining the project planning and control system requirements. The second step takes these general requirements and restructures them in the form of a detailed system specification. The final step is the development of each procedure from the specification. Each procedure contains a logic diagram, narrative text, and instruction related to the fulfillment of the procedure requirements.

DPC is currently engaged with XXXXXXXXXXXXXXXXXXXXXXXXX-XXXXXXXXXXXXXXXXX to develop a customized training program on project planning and control concepts. This program is based on DPC's public seminar, which is currently being presented nationwide. DPC has, however, made substantial changes in the presentation material to be XXXXXXXXXXXXX-specific. This training program provides a perfect base for developing system procedures. Having DPC execute the proposed procedures development program will assure XXXX of maximizing its investment in the training program and make procedure implementation much easier.

1.2 Proposed Services

Decision Planning Corporation offers to accomplish the scope of work outlined below and defined in the Technical Proposal. To assure a clear and complete understanding of the work scope between XXXXXXX-XXXXXX and DPC, the proposed program has been subdivided into its component parts by means of a Program Work Breakdown Structure (PWBS) shown in Figure 1. Following is a brief description of the elements of this scope at the second level of the DPC PWBS.

WBS ELEMENT 1   *Project Planning and Control System Review*: WBS Element No. 1 includes: a review of the existing XXXXXXXXXXXXXXXXXXXXXXXXX-XXXXXXXXXXXXXXXXX Project Planning and Control (PP&C) System documentation to gain an understanding of the current XXXX project planning and control techniques; a survey of sample XXXX projects to assure a clear understanding of planning and

Figure 1

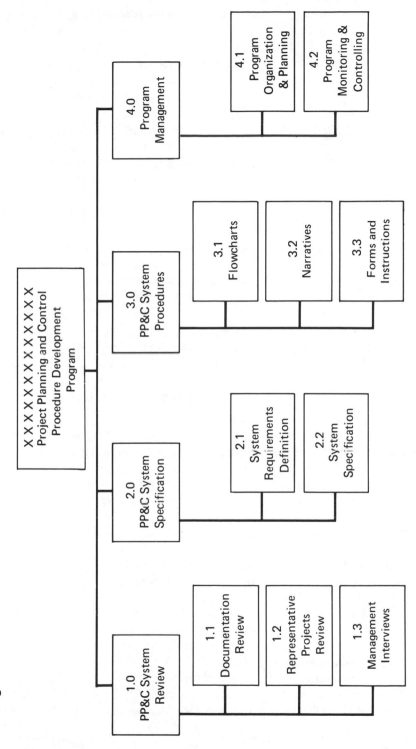

	control needs of projects by size and type; and interviews with XXXX management personnel to understand unwritten practices, procedures, working relationships, and attitudes.
WBS ELEMENT 2	*Project Planning and Control Systems Specification*: This WBS element includes activities related to defining requirements for organizing, planning, authorizing, monitoring, and controlling project work and resources, and preparation of a specification that will be the basis for preparing each procedure.
WBS ELEMENT 3	*Project Planning and Control Procedures*: This WBS contains development of system procedures, including system flow diagrams, procedure narratives, and forms design and completion instructions.
WBS ELEMENT 4	*DPC Program Management*: This WBS element includes the organizing, planning, monitoring, and controlling of the work and resources necessary to assure the successful and timely completion of this engagement.

A detailed description of each WBS element is provided in Section 2, Technical Proposal. An overview of the approach DPC proposes for accomplishing the program work is shown in Figure 2. DPC's work methodology is described in the form of a logic diagram depicting the relationship of WBS subelements. In Section 4.0, this logic diagram was used as a basis for development of a realistic program schedule.

1.3   Decision Planning Corporation Qualifications

Decision Planning Corporation has an outstanding record in the field of project management. Formed in 1972, Decision Planning Corporation has built a nationwide consulting practice and provided services to over 100 organizations from a variety of industries and several branches of the Federal Government. Among DPC's clients are electric utilities, construction companies, architectural/engineering firms, reactor manufacturers, aerospace/defense contractors, the U.S. Departments of Energy and Defense, the Canadian Federal Government, and many other organizations. These organizations received assistance from Decision Planning Corporation in virtually every aspect of project management. Appendix A indi-

Figure 2

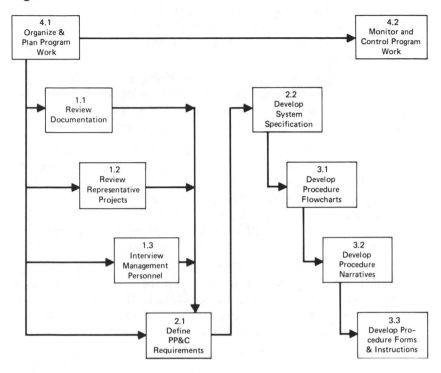

cates the extent of DPC experience in the areas of project management relevant to this proposal. Of special interest to XXXXXXXXXXXXX is the assistance provided to the Bonneville Power Administration, the Northwest Energy Corporation, the General Public Utilities Services Company, the Gas-Cooled Reactor Associates, and Southern Company Services. These engagements were performed in essentially the same environment and included the same scope of work as described in this proposal.

DPC personnel possess diverse experience in all aspects of project management, ranging from participation in the development of original concepts of Integrated Project Management, to achieving remarkable results in the management of projects utilizing these concepts. For this proposed work, Decision Planning Corporation has selected a team of experienced project management professionals. Each has extensive experience in project management control systems design, documentation, training, implementation, and operation.

Their experience will assure that the XXXXXXXXXXXXXXXXXXX-XXXXXXXXXXXXXXX Project Planning and Control System Procedures will reflect the needs of the company and will be the correct combination of proper structure and practical knowledge of the needs of the project manager/engineer.

Decision Planning Corporation is uniquely qualified to assist XXXXXXX-XXXXXXXX XXXXXXXXXXXXXXXXXX on this program. Following is a summary of the benefits that will accrue to XXXXXXXXXXXXXX by selecting Decision Planning Corporation for this assignment.

- DPC is intimately familiar with the XXXXXXXXXXXXXXXXXXX-XXXXXXXXXXXXX project management environment. By selecting Decision Planning Corporation for this assignment, XXXX will gain the benefit of DPC's extensive experience in the design, documentation, implementation, and operation of project management systems, thereby assuring that the PP&C procedures effort will be accomplished expeditiously.

- DPC is an expert in Project Planning and Control techniques of the Electric Utility Industry. DPC offers, as perhaps the only one of its kind in the United States, a public seminar entitled, "Project Planning and Control Within the Electric Utility Industry." XXXX will gain the benefit of this know-how and experience in this engagement.

- Decision Planning Corporation personnel contemplated for this assignment possess a balance of business and engineering backgrounds, thereby providing the disciplines necessary to conceptualize the system, utilizing a project manager's awareness of what is practical and what is not.

- Decision Planning Corporation experience with project management assignments in the project planning and control environment has extreme depth and breadth. Over the past five years, Decision Planning Corporation has assisted 20 major organizations involved in engineering/construction activities in the development, implementation, and operation of project management.

- Decision Planning Corporation's entire corporate mission is dedicated to the business of assisting clients in the design, implementation, and operation of project management systems. Therefore, this effort is not secondary to other Decision Planning Corporation services. It is the central focus of its corporate experience and expertise.

In order to support the statements made and confirm the capabilities and performance records of Decision Planning Corporation, the following is

7

a list of references provided to XXXXXXXXXXXXXXXXXXXXXXXXXXXX-XXXXXXX for review.

[List of references intentionally deleted.]

2.0 TECHNICAL PROPOSAL

Decision Planning Corporation proposes to provide the necessary services and related support to XXXXXXXXXXXXXXXXXXXXXXXXXXXXXXXX-XXXX in the conduct of a management system procedure development program outlined below. The program scope is presented in a modular fashion to enable XXXX to identify how those services are best suited to its present management needs.

SCOPE

The proposed scope of work involves the performance of ten (10) specific tasks. The individual tasks are structured as elements of a Work Breakdown Structure as shown in Figure 1. The purpose of the Work Breakdown Structure is to define the deliverable products and services necessary to complete the program scope and to assure that the management of the engagement WBS is coded by a unique identification number. This number is used to identify the WBS element on all cost and schedule documents contained in this proposal. By using the WBS identification number, XXXX may correlate all proposed cost and schedule information to the work scope defined for that element.

RESPONSIBILITIES

Since the WBS describes the products and services associated with management system procedure development, and not the responsibility for preparing the product or performing the service, an identification of the responsibilities for various tasks regarding each individual WBS element product/service is set forth in Figure 3, Responsibility Matrix. The matrix contains the following information.

- The vertical axis provides a listing of all WBS elements, products, and services.

8

Figure 3

Responsibility Matrix		Responsible Organization							
		DPC				XXXX			
Work Breakdown Structure Element		Execute	Review	Consult		Execute*	Review	Approve	
Number	Description								
1.0	PP&C System Review								
1.1	Documentation Review	x							
1.2	Representative Project Review	x				x			
1.3	Management Interviews	x				x			
2.0	PP&C System Specification								
2.1	System Requirements Definition	x		x		x		x	
2.2	System Specification	x				x		x	
3.0	PP&C System Procedures								
3.1	Flowcharts	x	x			x	x	x	
3.2	Narrative	x	x			x	x	x	
3.3	Forms and Instructions	x	x			x	x	x	
4.0	Program Management								
4.1	Program Organization & Planning	x						x	
4.2	Program Monitoring and Control	x						x	

*XXXX effort is expected to take one equivalent person.

- The horizontal axis contains a listing of activities associated with product/service development.
- Where axes intersect, a symbol is used to indicate responsibility for performance of the activity under consideration.

9

Activities associated with accomplishment of the proposed scope of work are identified as *execution*, *review*, *consulting*, and *approval*. Statements shown below describe program activities in terms of the content of work and deliverable products, where applicable.

EXECUTE

System review and analysis, flowchart preparation, development of procedures, and their presentation to the XXXX personnel. All executed activities have clearly defined end products and/or services.

REVIEW

Analysis of results of execution activities for completeness and adequacy. Results of all reviews will be documented on the marked-up copies of program documentation, through memoranda, or by means acceptable to the XXXX and DPC.

CONSULTING

Activities related to advisory program administration, management, and other "level of effort" work that does not result in a tangible end product.

APPROVAL

Work associated with formal acceptance of various products and services by the XXXX-XXXXXXXXXXXXXXXX XXXXXXXXXXX.

Decision Planning Corporation believes that material contained in this proposal presents a precise definition of the scope of work and responsibilities for its execution. It should be noted that the proposal quantifies the program scope to the maximum practical extent and avoids level of effort activities wherever possible. This provides a sound basis for management of the DPC work scope and assures adequate visibility into the progress of each product.

2.1 WBS Element 1.0—Project Planning and Control (PP&C) System Review

Decision Planning Corporation will review XXXXXXXXXXXXXXXXXXX-XXXXXXXXXXXXXXX's PP&C System documentation, survey its project plans and reports, and conduct interviews with XXXX management personnel, as needed. This effort will involve a three-step process. Each step is described below.

WBS ELEMENT 1.1   *PP&C Documentation Review*: DPC will review existing PP&C documentation and
"take inventory" of current XXXX practices
associated with organizing, planning, authorizing, monitoring, and controlling labor,
materials, and associated resources. This "inventory" will consist of the following:
  a. Review of organization charts and po-
     sition descriptions to develop an under-
     standing of rules and responsibilities of
     people and organizations, and to iden-
     tify the key interfaces of various project
     participants.
  b. Review of other management policies,
     procedures, manuals, and related docu-
     mentation to gain familiarity with cur-
     rent PP&C methods and practices.
  c. Review of existing accounting and
     information systems to develop an un-
     derstanding of: (1) labor distribution;
     (2) procurement/material commit-
     ments and distribution; (3) other direct
     costs distribution; and (4) other perti-
     nent project and accounting informa-
     tion resources.

WBS ELEMENT 1.2   *XXXX Project Review*: DPC will review the
character of the current engineering, construction, and maintenance projects. The review will consider a sample drawn from each
of the major project groups—fossil plants,
hydro plants, and transmission lines. The
sample will be used to profile the project
management requirements of XXXX projects
of each type and size. The review will address,
as a minimum, the following:

  a. Work Breakdown Structure and other
     project definition documents as pres-
     ently exist.
  b. Schedules throughout all levels.
  c. Budget and/or expenditure forecasting
     documents.

11

      d. Work authorization documents, including contracts and purchase orders.

      e. Work progress/accomplishment and problem analysis document/reports.

WBS ELEMENT 1.3   *Management Interviews*: Decision Planning Corporation will hold interviews with managers and other key personnel in engineering, project services, and other appropriate functional management areas to gain understanding of unwritten practices and procedures, working relationships, and relevant attitudes.

2.2 WBS Element 2.0—Project Planning and Control System Specification

Decision Planning Corporation will develop a specification for the enhancement of the XXXX Project Planning and Control System. This specification will define criteria for organizing, planning, monitoring, and controlling project work and resources, and analyze XXXX practices against these criteria.

WBS ELEMENT 2.1   *PP&C System Requirements Definition*: DPC (with the assistance of XXXX) will analyze project management practices identified in WBS Element 1.0 in light of existing project management requirements, and identify any additional requirements, as well as those which require further development. This approach will assure that the PP&C system reflects the state-of-the-art in project management thought, as well as management style, values, and philosophy of the XXXX.

WBS ELEMENT 2.2   *System Specification*: The results of the system requirements analysis will be documented in a System Specification. The specification will contain project management requirements and identity of the priorities that should govern the PP&C System procedure development. The report will also document the satisfactory features of the existing management systems so that eventual system modification effort can be undertaken with minimum change to existing practices.

2.3   WBS Element 3.0—PP&C System Procedures

Following the documentation of XXXX system requirements, DPC, with XXXX assistance, will prepare the system procedures that meet those requirements.

WBS ELEMENT 3.1   *Flowcharts*: DPC and XXXX will prepare graphic flowcharts of the existing management practices. These flowcharts will be compared to the requirements in the System Specification. Any shortcomings will be resolved jointly between DPC and XXXX. The outcome will be a flowchart of each intended procedure in the PP&C System. These flowcharts will identify existing practices, modified practices, and any new practices and forms required to implement the practice. Upon completion of the flowcharts, narrative explanations (text) of each step will be prepared. The flowcharts and narratives will allow each reviewer to understand the flow and interaction of each step by viewing the graphical flowchart and understanding the contents of each step through review of the adjacent narrative. The ultimate goal is to assure that each intended procedure has considered and clarified all necessary steps and interfaces.

A preliminary list of minimal system documentation follows:

- PP&C System Overview
- Work Definition and Responsibility Assignment Matrix
- Project Budgeting
- Project Scheduling Procedure
- Control Point Plan Development Procedure
- Authorizing Procedure
- Performance Measurement Procedure

13

- Baseline Measurement Procedure
- Analysis and Forecasting Procedure
- Change Control/Revision Procedure
- Control Point Manager's Guide

The complete/final list of procedural documentation will be identified prior to any procedure development work. Each procedure will contain a flow diagram, flow diagram narrative, existing forms and/or new forms, narrative describing the purpose and scope of the procedure, definition of unique or new terms, and procedure requirements.

WBS ELEMENT 3.2   *Procedure Narratives*: Utilizing the flowchart narratives, DPC, with XXXX assistance, will prepare the series of procedures which will totally define the PP&C System.

WBS ELEMENT 3.3   *Forms and Instructions*: DPC will, if necessary, develop/revise PP&C forms and form instructions to be compliant with system procedure requirements. This task includes developing preliminary drafts, coordinating and reviewing preliminary drafts, and developing final drafts of both forms and form instructions.

2.4   WBS Element 4.0—Overall Program Management

In order to assure successful and timely completion of the proposed effort, this program must be organized, planned, monitored, and controlled effectively. The scope of work described below is designed to accomplish the above goals.

WBS ELEMENT 4.1   *Program Organization and Planning*: Near the outset of the program, DPC will finalize the following documents and submit them to XXXX for review:

- Work Breakdown Structure   (Figure 1)
- Organization Structure   (Figure 3)
- Detailed Program Execution Network   (Figure 2)
- Program Schedule   (Figure 6)

14

These documents will be designed to assure that all project activities have been thoroughly defined, assigned, and planned, and that adequate manpower is available for their accomplishment.

WBS ELEMENT 4.2   *Program Monitoring and Control*: DPC will continuously monitor the cost and progress of the program work and performance of DPC personnel. DPC recognizes that, during the execution of this program, a need may develop to alter the program scope, schedule, and/or budget. DPC will montior the need for such changes, present them formally to XXXX management, and mutually agree upon the course of corrective action.

3.0   COST PROPOSAL

3.1   Estimate of Cost Elements

As described in Section 2.0, DPC has subdivided the XXXXXXXXXX-XXXXXXXXXX XXXXXXXXXX PP&C Procedure Development Program through three (3) levels of the WBS. The activities necessary to accomplish the statements of work were scheduled in a manner that considers the relationships and interdependencies of the various work elements.

DPC's cost estimate to perform the work described in Section 2.0 is shown in Figures 4 and 5. The figures show the labor and other resources necessary to accomplish each element of the DPC WBS. The labor categories depicted are: Director of Projects, Senior Consultant, and Consultant. Estimates are shown in manhours by labor category.

Decision Planning Corporation developed its cost estimate based on the labor rates shown below. [Note that the rates have been intentionally deleted.] These rates are based upon uniform market prices for services provided in substantial quantity to the general public. DPC labor rates are:

Director of Projects	/day
Senior Consultant	/day
Consultant	/day

The above rates are valid only for the resources shown and for a period of five months. If, during the course of this engagement, DPC is requested

15

Figure 4

Estimate by Cost Elements	Labor*			Other				
	Director of Projects	Senior Consultants	Consultants	Airfare	Hotel/ Per Diem (Days)	Car Rental (Days)	Parking (Days)	Misc.
1.1 Documentation Review	8	8	10					
1.2 Representative Project Review	8	8	10					
1.3 Management Interview	8	8	12					
1.0 Total Review	24	24	32	3	13	5	13	3
2.1 System Requirement Definition	12	40	8					
2.2 System Specification	12	16	8					
2.0 Total System Specification	24	56	16	2	10	5	10	2
3.1 Procedure Flowcharts	4	80	120					
3.2 Procedure Narratives	3	120	160					
3.3 Procedure Forms and Instructions	3	40	56					
3.0 Total Procedures	10	240	336	9	43	24	43	9
4.1 Program Organization & Planning	16	24	12					
4.2 Program Monitoring & Controlling	16	24	12					
4.0 Total Program Management	32	48	24	2	10	5	10	2
Total Program	90	368	408	16	76	39	76	16

*Labor estimate is in manhours.

Note: Use or disclosure of the data set forth hereon is subject to the restriction on the cover page of this proposal.

to provide services requiring special expertise in areas other than project planning and control, billing rates for such services will be negotiated with XXXX at that time.

Other cost elements shown are estimated in units appropriate to the cost element. The cost elements and the units estimated are as follows:

Figure 5

Estimated Cost for Proposed Services	Quantity/Cost	Labor				Other Cost Elements						Total Price
WBS Element	Q / $ (Unit Price (Hr))	Director of Projects	Senior Consultants	Consultants	Staff Consultants	Airfare	Hotel/ Per Diem	Car Rental (Days)	Parking (Days)	Mileage (100 mi.)	Visual Aids	
1.0 PP&C System Review	Q / $	24	24	32		3	13	5	13	3		
2.0 PP&C System Specification	Q / $	24	56	16		2	10	5	10	2		
3.0 PP&C System Procedures	Q / $	10	240	336		9	43	24	43	9		
4.0 Program Management	Q / $	32	48	24		2	10	5	10	2		
Total Program												

[Rates and costs intentionally deleted.]

Cost Elements	Unit of Estimation
Airfares	Roundtrips from Costa Mesa to ZZZZZZZ
Hotel/Per Diem	Days × number of on-site consultants
Car Rental	Days × number of cars rented
Parking	Days × number of cars parked
Miscellaneous	Dollars per trip

At present, DPC anticipates that the only materials that may be required are the general office supplies, light graphics, and reproduction.

3.2 Cost Estimate Rationale

The cost estimate for the proposed services is based upon the following assumptions:

- Timely completion and total cost of this program are dependent on the strict adherence of all participants to the project schedule.

- XXXX will provide office space and all necessary facilities for the DPC personnel while engaged in on-site activities. On-site activities include approximately 60% of the total effort.

- The term "site" refers to the XXXX offices located at ZZZZZZZZZZZ ZZZZZZZZZZZZZZZ. Travel to locations other than the "site" shall be regarded as out-of-scope activity and shall be negotiated/billed separately.

- Total project duration is assumed to be 10–12 weeks.

- DPC currently reimburses its personnel for lodging at cost and provides a food and incidentals allowance rate of ___ per day. For the ZZZZZZZ area, DPC estimates ___ per night, which represents the middle range of a single hotel room. The total of ___ per day has been multiplied against the estimated number of per diem days. [Rates and costs have been intentionally deleted.]

- Substantial cost savings can be realized by taking advantage of airline discounts and/or price reductions. However, to take advantage of these reductions, a firm schedule must be established. As soon as a firm schedule is established, DPC will attempt to take advantage of all possible cost savings related to travel, reducing the overall travel-related expenses.

3.3 Cost Summary

The cost estimate for the proposed statement of work associated with procedure development has been summarized in Figure 5. The total cost estimate is for all services/products described in Section 2.0. [Cost has been intentionally deleted.]

3.4 Invoice and Payment

DPC will invoice XXXXXXXXXXXXXXXXXXXXXXXXXXXXXXXXX each month for the costs incurred at the billing rates and actual expense costs incurred to date. (Refer to Figure 6, Program Schedule.) DPC anticipates payment will be received from XXXX within 30 days of submission of the invoice.

All payments should be made to:

> Decision Planning Corporation
> 3184-A Airway Avenue
> Costa Mesa, California 92626

4.0 MANAGEMENT PROPOSAL

This section describes the organizational approach that DPC uses on its consulting assignments, the specific team proposed for this program, and the schedule for accomplishing the statement of work.

4.1 Program Organization and Staffing

Decision Planning Corporation controls all of its assignments with a matrix organization as shown in Figure 7, DPC Organization. The left side of this chart depicts DPC officers, and the right side shows the organization of the Program Team.

DPC will appoint Mr. Richard Brodkorb as Director of this program to provide for adequate interfacing with XXXX management and to assure complete control of project resources. Mr. Brodkorb will be supported by a team that possesses a unique blend of technical and business management backgrounds chosen specifically for this assignment. All team members will not be utilized at the same rate; three team members are proposed in order to assure that qualified individuals are available to support peak periods. A synopsis of the proposed team members and their experience related to this assignment is presented below. A more detailed resume on each member is included in Appendix B.

[Synopses intentionally deleted.]

19

Figure 6

PROPOSED SCHEDULING FOR XXXXXXXXXXXXXXXXXXXXXXXXXXXX
PROJECT PLANNING & CONTROL PROCEDURE DEVELOPMENT

ACTIVITY		WEEKS FROM START											
NO.	DESCRIPTION	1	2	3	4	5	6	7	8	9	10	11	12
1.1	Documentation Review	▊											
1.2	Representation Project Review	▊											
1.3	Management Interview	▊											
2.1	System Requirement Definition		▊										
2.2	System Specification		▊	▊									
3.1	Flowcharts				▊	▊	▊	▊	▊				
3.2	Narratives				▊	▊	▊	▊	▊	▊			
3.3	Forms and Instruction				▊	▊	▊	▊	▊	▊			
4.1	Program Organization & Planning	▊	▊	▊	▊	▊	▊	▊	▊	▊	▊		
4.2	Program Monitoring and Controlling	▊	▊	▊	▊	▊	▊	▊	▊	▊	▊		

Figure 7

DPC ORGANIZATION

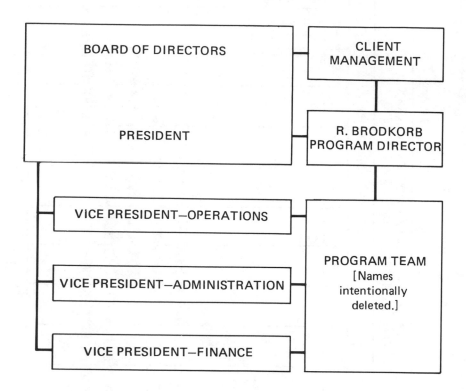

4.2   Staffing Restrictions

The proposed staff is available to support XXXXXXXXXXXXXX within three weeks of the date of this proposal. However, should authorization to proceed be delayed beyond November 15, 1985, DPC may be required to assign a portion of the proposed personnel to other engagements. If this occurs, DPC will replace the reassigned personnel with staff members of equal qualifications. Replacements will be made with the approval of XXXXXXXXXXXXXXXXXXXXXXXXXXXXXXXXXX.

4.3   Program Schedule

The proposed schedule for accomplishment of the XXXX Project Planning and Control Procedure Development Program is shown in Figure 6. The

21

schedule was developed in the framework of the Work Breakdown Structure (Figure 1), and it depicts time-phasing and duration of all activities identified in the Execution Logic Diagram (Figure 2).

Rather than being oriented toward specific calendar dates, the schedule is constructed based upon working days and weeks after commencement of the engagement. A minimum of two weeks advance notice should be given in order for DPC to support desired dates.

INDEX

ABOUT THE AUTHOR

Dr. William A. Cohen is Professor of Marketing and Associate Chairman of the Marketing Department and the Director of the Small Business Institute at California State University at Los Angeles. He is on several boards of directors and is the author of 12 business books. His seminars on consulting, marketing, and management have been presented internationally. He developed a special upper-division academic course in consulting that he currently teaches at California State University at Los Angeles. He was designated "Outstanding Professor" for 1982–83, only the second business professor to be so honored since the award was established in 1963.

As President of his own consulting firm and Director of the Small Business Institute, he consults for *Fortune* 500 companies and small businesses, as well as for the United States government. He is the recipient of numerous awards and grants and is listed in numerous *Who's Who*s. Dr. Cohen is a member of the American Marketing Association and the Direct Marketing Association and a fellow of the Academy of Marketing Science. He has a BS degree in engineering from the United States Military Academy, an MBA from the University of Chicago, and an MA and PhD in management from Claremont Graduate School.